Fat Girl Best Friend

'Claiming Our Space'
Plus Size Women in Film & Television

Sarah Grant

TIPPERMUIR
· BOOKS LIMITED ·

Fat Girl Best Friend – Sarah Grant
Copyright © 2023. All rights reserved.

The right of Sarah Grant to be identified as the author of the Work has been asserted in accordance with the Copyright, Designs & Patents Act 1988.

This first edition published and copyright 2023 by
Tippermuir Books Ltd, Perth, Scotland.

mail@tippermuirbooks.co.uk – www.tippermuirbooks.co.uk.

ISBN 978-1-913836-21-4 (paperback).

A CIP catalogue record for this book is available from the British Library.

Project coordination and editorial by
Paul S Philippou, Rosa Maria Alexander and Julia Garcia.

Cover design by Molly Hankinson.

Cover coordination: Matthew Mackie.

Editorial support: Ajay Close, Steve Zajda and Jean Hands.

Co-founders and publishers of Tippermuir Books: Rob Hands,
Matthew Mackie and Paul S Philippou.

Text design, layout, and artwork by Bernard Chandler [graffik].
Text set in Bliss 9.5/12pt with Marker Felt titling.

Printed and bound by Ashford Colour Press.

Fat Girl Best Friend

We all want to live our lives with oodles of Main Character Energy, but for some of us, we just don't look like your average 'entertainment thin' Leading Lady.

Whilst we live in an age of body positivity, we are not seeing that reflected in the cinema or on our television screens. From Fat Monica to Fat Amy, plus size women in film and television are a rare commodity, and even when we do see ourselves represented at all, it's not a pretty picture. We're either the pitied bully victim or the empty, sympathetic and disposable best friend.

Through the lens of Female Friendship, *Fat Girl Best Friend* dives into the treatment of plus size women in film and television, and goes looking for that Main Character Energy we all know we deserve.

In Fat Girl Best Friend, Sarah Grant, a queer writer, filmmaker, actor and poet – takes the reader on a film and television voyage which encompasses *Bird Box, Booksmart, Bridesmaids, Bridgerton, Bridget Jones Diary, Castle Rock, Crazy Ex-Girlfriend, Cyrano de Bergerac, The DUFF, Dumplin, Empire, Encanto, Eternal Sunshine of the Spotless Mind, Ever After, Falling for Figaro, Friends, Gavin and Stacy, Gilmore Girls, Glee, Hairspray, Halloween, Harry Potter and the Philosopher's Stone, I Feel Pretty, Insatiable, Inside Out, Just Wright, Lady Bird, The Lion King, The Little Mermaid, Love Actually, Matilda, Midsommar, House of Wax, Mike and Molly, My Mad Fat Diary, Misery, Orphans, Orange is the New Black, Pitch Perfect, Pride and Prejudice, Schitts Creek, Shallow Hal, She-Ra and the Princesses of Power, Shrek, Shrek 2, Sierra Burgess is a Loser, Sleeping Beaty, Star Wars, Stranger Things, The Sword and the Stone, Turning Red, The Vicar of Dibley, Unbelievable, What to Expect When You're Expecting.*

About the Author

Sarah is a working-class writer, filmmaker, and poet from Glasgow. She has made numerous BAFTA qualifying short films, and numerous comedy sketches for BBC Scotland, featuring body and sex positive female-fronted comedy (one of which won a Royal Television Society Scotland award) and gained tens of millions of views across digital and social media.

She is currently taking steps towards creating long-form film and television work, having developed a feature script with Short Circuit and Screen Scotland through their First Features programme, and partaking in programmes such as the Edinburgh International Film Festival Talent Lab and UKTV Comedy 50:50 pilot initiative.

Sarah is the co-writer of new BBC Scotland comedy 15-minute pilot, 'STUNNERS'. Sarah is committed to body positive, sex positive and inclusive female-led stories that are honest, feminist and fearless.

https://www.sarahgrantcreative.com

'[Sarah Grant is] *The Future of Scottish Comedy.*' 'Ooh the Banter', **BBC One Scotland** (Hogmanay Broadcast 2023)

'Sarah is not only one of our best filmmakers she is Scotland's rising star, having won national awards and acclaim.'
Sam Goldblatt, Capital Theatres & 48 Hour Film Project

Sarah Grant's 'Candy' is a heartening body positive reclamation of sexuality and empowerment'.
Directors Notes

'Full of charm, humour and bright observations, Sarah Grant handles political weight with ease. Her writing advocates for a world of gorgeous gallus-ness where every woman can flourish as the protagonist of her own chosen story.'
Catherine Wilson, Poet & Writer

For Katrina

The 'Amy' to my 'Molly'

'Who allowed you to take my breath away?!'

Content Warning and Spoilers

This book contains infrequent references to the following themes that some readers might find upsetting: violence, threat, sexual abuse, fatphobia, eating disorders, mental health issues, alcohol/drug misuse, abortion, homophobia, racism and abuse.

Please practise self-care before, during and after reading.

This book also deep dives into several properties across film and television. This is a blanket spoiler warning for the following shows: *Bird Box, Booksmart, Bridesmaids, Bridgerton, Bridget Jones Diary, Castle Rock, Crazy Ex-Girlfriend, Cyrano de Bergerac, The DUFF, Dumplin, Empire, Encanto, Eternal Sunshine of the Spotless Mind, Ever After, Falling for Figaro, Friends, Gavin and Stacy, Gilmore Girls, Glee, Hairspray, Halloween, Harry Potter and the Philosopher's Stone, I Feel Pretty, Insatiable, Inside Out, Just Wright, Lady Bird, The Lion King, The Little Mermaid, Love Actually, Matilda, Midsommar, House of Wax, Mike and Molly, My Mad Fat Diary, Misery, Orphans, Orange is the New Black, Pitch Perfect, Pride and Prejudice, Schitts Creek, Shallow Hal, She-Ra and the Princesses of Power, Shrek, Shrek 2, Sierra Burgess is a Loser, Sleeping Beauty, Star Wars, Stranger Things, The Sword and the Stone, Turning Red, The Vicar of Dibley, Unbelievable, What to Expect When You're Expecting.*

Acknowledgments

I never thought I would write a book so getting me to this point took a hell of a lot of convincing, and endless support from the people around me. This would not have been possible without them, and I want to thank them here.

Firstly, my publishers, Paul Philippou and Rosa Maria Alexander, who saw my pitch for this book in tweet form as part of the #Expo-North and thought that there might be something in there. From that moment on, through every chat and chapter they have been the most insightful and kind team, convincing me at every stage that what I was writing about is actually important. I couldn't ask for better assassins of the imposter syndrome.

Dr Abbie Menzies, who has a literal doctorate in this subject and who sat with me over coffee and helped me take this big concept and focus in on a structure. She is the most generous person and her work is so important, I encourage everyone to follow her and read everything she writes.

Heather and Lorraine, (who I have affectionately started referring to as 'the aunts') who have throughout this process time and time again offered their home as a beautiful and safe space to come and work in when it felt like the city was stepping on my head.

Catherine Wilson, who is always up for deep diving into big ideas with me over Messenger and who was the first person to ask to read this book. I can't wait to send you a copy.

Caitlin Magnall-Kearns who provided beautiful insight and guidance with a difficult chapter when I couldn't see the wood for the trees.

Lorna, Jim and Hannah Grant, who are always supportive of me no matter what I do, even if I am still the arty-farty one of the family.

My husband, Dev, who has listened to many a ramble and rant and always knew exactly when to offer an opinion, a cuddle, a cup of tea or a companionable silence. You make everything better.

Molly Hankinson who designed the cover of my dreams, I can't believe we exist in the same universe, never mind the same project. I'm so lucky to have worked with you.

To Dawn French and Nicola Coughlan and Lizzo and Melissa McCarthy and Jo Brand and Queen Latifah and all the other women daring to take up space in this industry; it's because of you I got this far, thank you for holding the door open behind you.

And finally, to Katrina, Nicola and Charlotte, the Taco Tuesday girls, and the wider Taco Tuesday community and filmmaking scene, who have made my year the best one ever. In whose love and company I always feel full.

CHAPTER 1
Beginnings

It's Christmas, 2006. I'm halfway through my one-year Film and Media National Qualification course at college. My UCAS application recently sent off, I await a response as to whether I have received a place to study Film, Media and English Studies at the University of Stirling.

I have my sights on one day being a writer and director for film and television.

Christmas Day is a quiet affair at my place. We stop by my granny's and my aunt's, say hello, exchange cuddles and presents, and then we go home and phone for a Chinese takeaway. An unusual Christmas tradition, but we do all pack onto the living room couch and watch the seasonal programming on the good ol' BBC.

The highlight of 2006: *The Vicar of Dibley Christmas Special*.

I was always a creative kid, but my decision to study Film at university came about after I saw Baz Luhrmann's 2001 musical explosion *Moulin Rouge*. Since I can remember, my sister and I have had freakish memories when it comes to movies. After seeing a film once, we could quote 90% of the script back to you. They were a huge part of my life and how I communicated with the world. Before the meme there was the movie quote. Despite this, it wasn't until my teens that I had a eureka moment that there was someone, an actual human person, whose job it was to decide why there were songs in *Moulin Rouge*, decide on the costumes, someone to read a script and bring it to life with their own brand of magic.

I wanted to be the person who made those choices.

I couldn't wait to get out into the world, move away for university and make memories. I had heard the phrase 'write what you know', but I was a working-class and sheltered kid, I didn't know much about anything. I knew Glasgow, I knew school, I knew the working-class family.

I also knew female friendships can save your life.

The Vicar of Dibley was familiar. I was raised on it. It was home. Geraldine 'Gerry' Granger – portrayed by national treasure Dawn French, a self-proclaimed 'babe with a bob-cut and a magnificent bosom' was a voice I knew very well. The show first aired in November 1994, a month before my sister was born, so technically I have known and loved Gerry longer than I have known and loved my sister. (I'll get some grief for making that comparison but it's worth it.)

The 2006 Christmas Special was to be the final episode, so I was sad to be saying goodbye to this formidable woman but excited to see the end of her story.

I should pause to tell you one very important thing here: *I am plus size*.

Since I was a pre-teen, it was very clear that I was growing into a 'big girl'. Development hit me like a double-decker bus. While some girls were getting their first bras, thanking the 'Gods of Puberty' for *finally* blessing them with B cups, I was crying into my GGs in the fitting rooms of John Lewis, begging my mother for surgery. My size has had such an impact on my life and therefore is a huge part of my identity.

Fat.

I know that the word 'fat' is an act of reclamation for some women – and more power to those women – but as someone who has been a Size 18 since they were eighteen and ridiculed throughout school for their weight, I'm not quite ready to cheerfully turn the language of my tormentors into a love language when referring to myself.

Not yet anyway. Maybe one day.

I think right now would be a good time to clarify that if I use either the term 'plus size' or 'fat' (I will switch between the two at various points), I am referring to someone who is not always able to buy clothing from the general sections of most High Street shops. As a UK Size 18, I am on the lower end of that spectrum but that has done nothing to dull the brutal barbs of blatant fatphobia throughout my life.

Now in my 30s, my body and I have been on quite a journey

together, not one without its ups and downs. As an adult I have had to do some unpicking of habits that were unhealthy and detrimental to my happiness, habits that were fostered by growing up surrounded by diet culture and unrealistic ideals of beauty perpetuated by the mainstream media. My confidence and I have an ever-changing and fluctuating relationship but for the most part it is a healthy one. Even on my worst days I can look at myself and feel love, and I know that my professional and personal worth are not tied to anyone's opinions on my exterior. It has taken a long time to get to this place of progress, and when I look back on that journey, I realise it is because my life has been filled with formative female friendships, and fierce female role models like Gerry Granger, a woman I saw from an early age taking up space, using her voice and making me laugh.

So, back to the Christmas Special. Gerry is complaining about the gentrification of the village of Dibley – that she's 'fed up of rich Londoners taking over our village...he can either get stuck in or sod off', and she makes her way over to Sleepy Cottage to tell the new owner exactly this...That is, until one such rich Londoner reveals himself to be sex on a stick: Harry the accountant, played by Richard Armitage. At this early point in Armitage's career, his most notable role to date was the leather-clad, smouldering baddie, Sir Guy of Gisborne, in the BBC's *Robin Hood*. To see him appear as the new man about Dibley made the Christmas Special extra festive for me. My heart damn near exploded out of my chest when he asked Gerry out on a date.

I was prepared for everything to go south. I had followed Gerry through all her failed sexual exploits over three seasons and two Christmas specials, and previous experience taught me to believe that things wouldn't go the way she wanted. But, after a whole episode of kissing (with tongues!), stalking him as he walked around the village with a mysterious pretty blonde girl (who turned out to be his sister) and a re-enactment of the classic jumping-in-to-the-deceptively-deep-muddy-puddle gag from Season One (this time with an added *Apocalypse Now* homage), Gerry is proposed to by the lovely Harry. She doesn't quite believe it herself, but when she is convinced of his proposal, she blurts out the infamous Emma Thompson at the end of *Sense and Sensibility* sound, before running through the village screaming in shock and joy. Honestly, I was ready to run with her.

To see this woman, this paragon of confidence and kindness, of sass and of self-proclaimed sexiness, get her happy ending (and with an utter *thirst trap* like Richard Armitage) was a formative moment for me. The perfect ending to a wonderful story. It armed me. It steadied me. It gave me purpose. It made me believe that not only could I be someone who told stories centring women like Geraldine Granger in my professional life, but I could also be as strong and as capable and vulnerable and loved as Gerry is in my personal life.

I wanted that kind of Main Character Energy.

I went into the new year ready for adulthood, for university, and for the start of my journey as a writer and filmmaker. Fuck, I was naive.

It's strange to think that the 2007 *Vicar of Dibley Christmas Special* was almost half my lifetime ago. I've grown up a lot since then, and I've used the latter half of my life pretty well.

I am a practising writer and director of film and television working in the Scottish Film and Media industry. I have a body of work I am proud of and a handful of awards (which doesn't mean much, but it helps me tell my imposter syndrome that I am, in fact, not shit), I'm kicking and screaming through this field, and I've made somewhat of a career of loudly speaking up for women (*all* women – none of your TERF nonsense here thank you) and our stories that are under-represented on screen.

Since Gerry Granger, there have been so few positive representations of women who look like me, and I am sick of it. I am a writer who is trying to put plus size women front and centre in their narratives without having to write characters who hate themselves, a director that is trying to walk the walk and set a good example for plus size actors, communicating that they will never be demoralised or treated as lesser in any of my narratives. That's behind-the-scenes stuff you don't need to know about. My work as a writer and director is not relevant to you or to this book. For the purpose of this book, I am one thing only.

I am you.

I am the audience. I'm the girl in the cinema; on the couch with a DVD; in bed watching television or anywhere with a device and a streaming service of my choice. I am a consumer of film and television. And, like all audiences, I am looking for something to connect to.

We enjoy and invest more in characters and stories if we relate to them. If you are a person with lived experience of war, films such as *Saving Private Ryan* and *Black Hawk Down* are going to hit you harder emotionally than it would someone without that experience. I personally don't think the girls in *Sex and the City* have any real problems and they need to invent them to make them seem interesting and not hyper-privileged and shallow, but I imagine if you're a rich woman from New York you would disagree with me.

Sadly, which will come as a shock to no one, the film and television landscapes have been rather dry of characters like Geraldine Granger. It's not as if they don't exist, far from it. There are some shining examples, but very few exhibit that Main Character Energy that I felt was promised to me when I watched the end of Gerry's story. In fact, when observing plus size women in film and television and comparing them, their characters and their stories, there is one recurring theme that keeps on rearing its ugly, unwelcome head. One narrative for plus size women, one role for them to be doomed to fulfil again and again and again.

THE FAT GIRL BEST FRIEND

Let's make life easier and use FGBF.

So many times I have smiled like an idiot when I see a pivotal role within a film or television show being portrayed by someone who looks like me. I reach for these characters, waiting for their stories, knowing I will probably in some way relate but I am kept waiting. My smile always fades quickly as whomever it is on screen is nothing more than a human-shaped prop, without any character development, wants, needs or goals set out in any screen time.

These are broad brushes to tar every plus size character in film and television and of course not all of them are FGBFs. But repeatedly I see these characters crop up as insipid wallflowers or sassy sidekicks, bolstering others while expecting no growth or development

5

of their own. It's not just the emptiness of these characters that infuriates me but how closely this ugly trope is intrinsically linked to female friendship on screen.

Female friendship is something that I have always been drawn to in my work because it has had such a big impact on my life. The girls with me through the worst of High School, the women who got me home safe on my most stupid of university blackouts and the women who held the door open for me professionally. The women who inspire me, who graft with me, who lift me, encourage me, share tacos and margaritas with me, who raise me and who love me. Despite being raised watching women on screen who look like me play the eternal sounding board or hopeless and naive, cling on to their best friends, when it comes to the women in my life, I have never once felt like I had to earn my place in their stories.

Well, this is my story. And, like I've said before, I am you, the audience. So, this is our story. As a writer and filmmaker, I want to create stories that will connect and resonate with people like me, but, as an audience member, all I want is to believe that there is space for such stories.

I'm just going to go ahead and say something that will make me sound like the Master of the Fucking Obvious, but here it is anyway: Hollywood and the Western media have always been the worst perpetrators of upholding and glorifying unrealistic body types, especially for women – presenting only the most limited scopes for ideal beauty and making the hundreds of millions of people who do not conform feel like shit for not upholding these unrealistic ideals. For a long time there were a very powerful few who controlled the mainstream media and how it reached the masses.

But a lot has changed since Gerry Granger's time. Social media and the internet have completely changed the rules of distribution; visibility and representation have never been better. Plus size model Tess Halliday has appeared on the cover of the top fashion magazines in the world, plus size influencers in everything from fashion to fitness are making full-time wages solely from being visible online. These real-life women are not waiting for permission to take up space in the world. It's just not quite being reflected yet on our screens.

Space is a powerful thing. Women are conditioned to take up as little of it as possible and as a plus sized woman, your very body is a painful reminder that you have failed. This toxic web of bullshit conditioning is something we are just starting to collectively unpick and expel from our consciousness.

Spending my life identifying with the FGBF taught me that my narratives were not as important as that of my Thin Friends, that I needed to earn my place in the circle, put their needs before my own and that I should naturally expect less than them in all things. It taught me to be grateful for second place. It is a toxic web that I am slowly unpicking from my brain. And it's working.

Plus size women in film and television are so few and far between, they stand far enough apart that you cannot see the similarities and the tropes that bind them and further perpetuate the negative stereotypes and subsequent treatment of plus size women. Through my lived experience and my training in both craft behind and in front of the camera, I am situated to see the similarities, no matter how distant they seem to be. These women characters are so inconsequential in the bigger picture of on-screen representation that who cares about tropes and stereotypes.

I care. And I'm done feeling like the FGBF. I want to be the Leading Lady. I want to embody that sweet and shining Main Character Energy.

I plan to take up space here on behalf of the plus size characters in film and television who were not given enough of it in their own stories – who faded into the background and were trotted out for a narrative purpose without ever being asked about their wants and goals.

Through the focused lens of female friendship, I am going to look closely at these characters outwith the context of their original texts, compare their journeys and their similarities. Maybe if we can give language to the behaviours of these characters it will be easier to call it out in the future. To demand more time, more information, more nuance and more development of the women sidelined. To demand more Main Character Energy.

CHAPTER 2

What is a Fat Girl Best Friend?

Not all fat women in film and television are the Best Friend character. Not all women Best Friend characters are fat. There are some (not many, but some) incredible examples of film and television where the lead character is a plus size woman. For every plus size Leading Lady with Main Character Energy, however, there are twenty FGBFs.

Every character is different, and every actor is different so it is hard to paint in such broad strokes in regards to this trope, but you cannot deny that time and time again when you see a plus size woman on screen (if you see one at all, they are still a very rare commodity) she will most likely be standing next to the main character, offering them selfless, sensible advice and support.

This is not a bad thing. There are many Best Friend characters that I would die for, no questions asked: Eric in *Sex Education*, Willow in *Buffy*, Sam in *Lord of the Rings*, all of them scene stealing sidekicks and audience favourites. All these characters have impacted me with their stories and their personalities and their struggles and hopes and fears, it's because of all those things that they are so moving and memorable.

But what about FGBF characters? Why haven't they had as much an impact on me as the above? I often find them unmemorable. There are three qualities that constitute a FGBF:

QUALITY 1: *FAT GIRL BEST FRIEND IS BEST FRIENDS WITH A LEAD CHARACTER WHO IS THIN*

This seems like an obvious one, but it's worth stating. Most of the time the friendships are established as old. We meet the Thin Lead and her FGBF and it is clear they have known each other *forever* and their relationship patterns are well established. Their friendship is what roots us in the ordinary world, making it one of the things that is disrupted when the story's inciting incident occurs.

Often in the narrative, the Thin Lead actively steers away from her routines and patterns in the name of character development. This includes her regular interaction with her FGBF. The Thin Lead will seek out a new sphere or situation that is subliminally suggested to be 'beyond' the FGBF.

The Thin Lead's ditching of her FGBF isn't usually played as intentional, it's often situational: the Thin Lead enters into a heteronormative relationship with a man, which reduces the contact between the friends; the Thin Lead joins a team, club or a sport that is exclusive or skill related which keeps the FGBF out.

Whether practical, situational or otherwise, there is a narrative line that the Thin Lead must cross on her journey that the FGBF 'cannot' cross with her.

QUALITY 2: *THE FAT GIRL BEST FRIEND HAS NO STAKE IN THE NARRATIVE OR CHARACTER DEVELOPMENT OUTSIDE OF HER FRIENDSHIP WITH THE THIN LEAD*

The FGBF is there for you 100% of the way. She does not have any substantial wants of her own.

Sure, maybe she has a line or two about wanting to do well in her exams, get out of her loveless marriage, work up the courage to wear a skirt, or something equally similar and banal, but none of her wants will be followed up on screen with any character development or space within the central narrative.

QUALITY 3: *THE FAT GIRL BEST FRIEND'S MAIN FUNCTION IS TO MOVE THE THIN LEAD IN THE RIGHT DIRECTION*

Whether through good advice, moral superiority or even out and out manipulation, the FGBF will make sure the Thin Lead gets her happy ending, no matter the cost. It's her most important job. There comes a time in every Thin Lead's story where she strays from the path and needs help to find her way back.

Whenever the Thin Lead has a crisis of confidence, they are spurred into action by the FGBF. Even if the action in question has some seriously questionable ethics, they will be convinced it is a good idea by the FGBF. In fact, the reason the Thin Lead hesitates at all is often because the action in question is so far from a normal reaction or choice that to have the Thin Lead suggest it herself would be damaging to her character. So, you need the FGBF to either deliver a sassy 'you go, girl' pep talk or a sad and mildly pathetic 'do it so I can live vicariously through you' emotional blackmail. If we need to engage in a little bit of questionable behaviour to move the story along at a structurally tight velocity, the FGBF will sanction it and convince the audience it is the right choice.

Exhibit A:

> TL: *My boyfriend says he loves me, but I'm worried he thinks I'm boring. I would look through his phone to see if he has been messaging other girls, but that's bad.*

> FGBF: *But you're amazing and doing it for the right reasons. Also, I don't have a boyfriend. After you leave, I will probably go cry somewhere.*

> TL: *You're so right. It is for the right reasons. I will invade his privacy. Thanks, FGBF.*

> FGBF: *Seeing you happy makes me forget that I'm going to die alone. I love you.*

> TL: *I love you too. Besties for life. Until I lock down this D. Then we can meet for brunch once every two months.*

You get the picture.

On the flip side, the FGBF will also alert the audience when the Thin Lead is making a wrong decision. They will act as a mirror, calling out the Thin Lead for her uncharacteristic behaviour and questioning whether her decisions are being made for the right reasons. This questioning of the Thin Lead's choices often puts the FGBF directly in the firing line, causing The Thin lead to break away from the friendship in order to do whatever she wants.

Exhibit B:

> TL: *He's cheating on me, I know it. I'm going to look through his phone and then sleep with his best friend.*

FGBF: *Or... And here me out here... Don't?*

TL: *I must! You don't understand!*

FGBF: *Okay, I've known you for literal de-cades, so I know you well enough to know you're having a crisis of confidence and lash-ing out because of your self-destructive ten-dencies. Again. Maybe don't?*

TL: *I hate you, FGBF! You are the reason my life is terrible! If I wasn't tied to you through the stupid bonds of friendship or whatever, I would be popular. Why won't you let me be popular?!*

FGBF: **sighs**

The Thin Lead will (eventually) either see the mistake of leaving her sphere and come back into the open and forgiving arms of her FGBF or she will thrive in her new environment and she and the former best friend will amicably acknowledge that they have outgrown each other. You can't even be mad at her, because the FGBF is so happy for her that her happiness is an endorsement of the Thin Lead's actions.

HOW DID THIS HAPPEN?

It's difficult to point a finger at who is responsible for perpetuating the FGBF trope but it just won't seem to die. In my career, I have read scripts where the only character descriptions are 'plump', 'overweight and messy' and 'corpulent' with no mention of person-ality. I've auditioned for roles that are written specifically for plus size women to then see the casting announcement with thin actors in the role. I've seen many things that are problematic in the treat-ment of plus size women but behind all those things were people, ignorant people, making decisions.

For the purpose of this book I will simply refer to the powers that are behind any examples mentioned as 'the creators' as it's impossible to know exactly who is to blame.

If by now you are still struggling to think of any characters that fit

11

the above description of a FGBF I really don't blame you. It's easy to miss something you rarely see in the foreground and are not looking for.

Fat Monica's fat suit might seem like a silly, throwaway joke. Fat Amy's out of control sexuality might seem progressive. The death of Barb caused the hashtag #JusticeforBarb to trend globally. Surely these are all good things, right? All representation is good representation, right?

I don't think so. Representation does not always need to be positive but it does need to be honest, and when the majority of plus size women on-screen are depicted as greedy, lazy and/or crazy caricatures it shows the creators have absolutely no care or respect for people who are living the plus size experience.

Plus size people are made to feel small, and often this applies to people who are not even plus size. It would be worth mentioning here that there are films that treat women who literally are not plus size as if they are, because they are not 'entertainment thin'. I would say anything above a UK Size 10 is not entertainment thin.

Even the advance of the body positive movement is not enough to combat diet culture, medical gaslighting and scapegoating, fear-mongering and the mainstream media circulating unrealistic and unattainable ideals of beauty and body. Society teaches you to not look too long at fat people because they are lazy, unmotivated and unattractive, so much so that it is *really* hard not to believe them.

I throw around words like 'society' and 'culture' a lot, and while I would love nothing more than to spend as much time as I have deep diving into the effect plus size women in film and television have on both these constructs, I need to concede that there will never be enough time or paper or audience attention span to cover everything that I want to.

The plus size experience does not live in a bubble, there are inter-sections of discrimination that overlap with fatphobia in ways that I, in my lived experience, cannot speak to. The way in which I experience fatphobia as a working-class, queer, white woman, will not be the same as how a non-binary person or a woman of colour might experience fatphobia. While I have attempted to be a broad in my exploring of this subject, I acknowledge there will be things I miss.

And that's okay. I am just one voice, here speaking and taking up space. My intention here is not only to make room for my story, but for all of our stories. We all deserve the space to tell our stories, they are important.

We, plus size people, have stories that are deserving of the big and small screen, and yet we so very rarely see ourselves represented in mainstream media.

As with everything, there is power in numbers. Maybe if several exemplary FGBFs from film and television stood next to each other it would be easy to see the similarities and discrepancies in each. It would be easier for them to point to their flaws and demand more from their creators. It would be easier for us, the audience, to do the same.

BONUS: *FAT GIRL BEST FRIEND BINGO*

Just for fun, here are a few things to look out for when you spot a plus size person in film and television from now on. Now, none of these things signify a FGBF, but they do represent a negative and stereotypical view of the plus size experience. The more of these bingo points that can be attributed to a single character, the more the writers reveal themselves to be lazy and reductive.

1. Physical Ineptitude – Falling down, being clumsy, having their physical body somehow get in the way of everyday activities such as bending down to pick up a phone, carrying things down a flight of stairs etc.

2. Frumpy Costuming – How much of the character's body can you see? Neckline? Upper arms? Are they covered from head to toe in a shapeless muumuu?

3. Holding/Talking About Food – Is the character always seen with a doughnut in their hand? Are they constantly talking about food or bringing it up in the most random

bits of dialogue? Are they eating on screen when no one else is? Bonus points if they eat messily or have food on their face.

4. Smacked Down Around Thin Lead – Does something happen when the FGBF and the Thin Lead are together to show the difference in their social status? Does someone smack the lunch tray out of the plus size character's hands? Or make a creepy comment about the size of her body? Or, alternatively, does another thin person approach the Thin Lead and talk to them/flirt with them while completely ignoring the presence of the FGBF?

5. Stating the Obvious – Does the FGBF say out loud, in whatever context, that she is fat? It doesn't need to have any kind of context. Bonus points if it is out of the blue.

6. Fat Boyfriend – If the FGBF has a romantic storyline (I'm mostly gearing this towards heteronormative romantic storylines), is her love interest also fat, or display other 'fat qualities' that alert the audience that the love interest is on a similar social standing as the FGBF (by which I mean low social standing).

If you keep these bingo points in your head as we move forward and start examining all the amazing plus size women to have graced film and television, you are bound to have a wild time. Oh, and if you wanna play in real time – there's a Bingo card at the back of the book that can be copied. Netflix/Amazon/Disney/Paramount Plus Size Bingo Binge Anyone?

CHAPTER 3

Young Adult

Is there a word for a fully grown adult who still adores YA fiction in all its formats?

Oh yes. A millennial.

I was a teenager at the height of *Twilight* fever, and also shared ages with the protagonists of *The Hunger Games*, *Mean Girls*, *Angus, Thongs and Full-frontal Snogging* and *The Sisterhood of the Travelling Pants*. These stories, the protagonists on the cusp of womanhood, the female friendships and the burning romances that never got any spicier than an accidental brushing of hands, had me and millions of others enslaved.

There's something about the stories that find us when we are teenagers that stay wrapped around our hearts for the rest of our lives.

As teenagers/young adults, we are starting to become the people we want to be. We dive into passions and interests. We wear our identities like the latest fashions and make choices that have rippling consequences. We make mistakes, over and over again.

Despite all this, the lives of teenagers are usually completely out of their control. They live with their parents or guardians and are financially dependent on whoever pays the bills in their household. They are afforded a glimpse of adult life that lies waiting for them when they are eighteen but are forced to sit in idleness and wait out the storm until adulthood brings with it freedom and autonomy.

And what better way to fill that time than with film and television? And what do most teenagers have in common? What shared experience can we all relate to as a basis for most YA stories?

High School.

I have chosen the YA genre as the first ground I intend to break on this venture for two reasons. The first is that it was at this time in my life I started to become aware of how the stories I was seeing on my screen could (and did) impact my life. The second is that

YA genre, specifically stories set against the backdrop of High School, is positively a breeding ground for the FGBF trope.

The FGBF trope isn't the only tired stereotype in the YA genre. There's the Regina George in *Mean Girls* Queen Bee trope, the Steve Harrington in *Stranger Things* Jock With a Soul trope, the Maeve Wiley in *Sex Education* Weirdo/'Slut' Everyone Secretly Fancies trope and the Patrick Verona in *10 Things I Hate About You* Bad Boy Who Turns Out to be Not That Scary trope. To name but a few.

With High School being an almost universal experience for teenagers it is an easy setting for any YA story. The audience already knows the structure of the day, the age ranges of the characters, the stakes and pitfalls of the students and the relationships between classmates, teachers and enemies. With so much of this taken for granted, it leaves the creators so much room in the script to play with the story they want to tell, leaning on the established structure whenever they need to and deviating whenever they want to.

This can be liberating, but it can also be lazy.

While these tropes have been used a million times, the reason we as an audience never really tire of them is that with each new iteration, each new character brings a freshness to the trope with interesting arcs, meaningful growth and ample screen time.

The FGBF trope is rarely afforded these luxuries.

From lived experience, I can say with all certainty that being a fat girl in High School is fucking horrible. It is extremely hard to have a good time when there is so much adversity and no escape from the social hierarchy narrative that deems you lesser than your thin counterparts. It's hard to feel anything but the stereotype when it is rammed down your throat at every turn.

But when all creators of YA stories lean into the stereotype for functionality and development of the script, is it possible to deviate from this tired and cruel depiction without having to completely reinvent the genre?

NEW YEAR NEW ME

Remember the first characteristic of the FGBF: be friends with a Thin Lead.

As awful as it is, we know that High School is an extremely hierarchical environment, so when the audience sees a fat girl character in a High School setting, they automatically assume that she has less social credit than her thin counterparts. We assume that this girl, whomever she is, is having a bad time. Because she is fat. And in High School. We collectively hold our breath for the moment the jock knocks her lunch tray out of her hands, calls her a name and walks away laughing, surrounded by a chorus of cronies.

If this sounds familiar then you probably also can recall that after this public bullying we usually see the Thin Lead tell her fat friend to just ignore them. This allying with the socially-disadvantaged fat girl signals to the audience that the Thin Lead is a good person; to act so charitably and to be kind enough to mentally exist outside of the High School hierarchy. In doing so, she also signals to the audience that she is not amongst the realms of the 'popular people', but she may be looking for a promotion.

No matter the sub-genre, the transformation from average to exceptional is essential in YA fiction. Of all the people in all the High Schools in all the world, what makes this one kid worthy of being the hero? Individuality is something to be desired: individuality can lead to being singled out as exceptional. Special.

Let's face it, in High School, we all wanted a glow up.

While for some lucky people it happens naturally – we all remember that one fifteen-year-old gangly boy in school who left for the summer and came back in the autumn buff as fuck, or a girl who grew out of her acne and got hips and tits almost overnight – for the rest of us a glow up moment needs to be pursued.

If we acknowledge that the FGBF character is representative of the lower ranks of the High School social hierarchy, then we acknowledge that the Thin Lead is voluntarily occupying the same rung of the ladder as her best friend. The most symbolic thing a Thin Lead can do to show she is ready for a glow up is to sacrifice her FGBF, to show she is willing to shrug off her old loser life that was keeping her down so she can transcend to the top of the social food chain.

It happens even in the most acclaimed and female driven stories. A classic example of this is Greta Gerwig's Oscar nominated directorial debut, the coming-of-age comedy-drama *Lady Bird*. Even this progressive, empowered and honest showcase of youth and womanhood sadly falls prey to the FGBF trope.

Christine 'Lady Bird' McPherson, played by Saoirse Ronan, is a High School senior, and the film revolves around her navigating her final days at her Catholic all-girls school and her strained relationship with her mother. Lady Bird wants to go to an East Coast school and get out of Sacramento. She is desperate to become more than she is – more cultured, more intelligent, more loved – and she is supported at every stage by her best friend, Julie Steffans, played by Beanie Feldstein.

While you could say that socially these two are equal, Julie may even have an advantage being cast as the lead in the school musical (Sondheim's *Merrily We Roll Along*) and having much better grades than Lady Bird, these are qualities that are not acknowledged by her best friend. Julie also has an overwhelming crush on a teacher that goes unnoticed by Lady Bird.

Julie is a slightly more nuanced FGBF: she deviates from some of the characteristics of the trope, as we see that she has wants and troubles of her own. She is shown to be a young woman with sexual desires when her and Lady Bird talk about masturbation while eating a jar of communion wafers (my favourite scene of the film). Both lie on the floor, legs propped up against the wall: the picture of childhood and innocence. The fact that they are talking about masturbation in this moment so perfectly reflects the tentative line between childhood and adulthood that young women on the verge of their sexual awakening walk, and it's a line that is not only reserved for young women who are thin. This nuanced and refreshing character work undertaken by Gerwig is undone by the dismissal and sacrificing of Julie's friendship by Lady Bird.

The lead character is insufferable. Her self-involvement and unappreciativeness of all that she has done for her is one of the main points of contention between her and her mother. Lady Bird is quite selfish, as acknowledged when she asks Julie to skip class because she had a free period and didn't want to be alone, often placing her own desires above anyone else in the room. Also, when she and Julie dance together at the Homecoming dance, she leaves Julie alone on the dancefloor to pursue Danny, not looking back or first making sure that her friend was okay and comfortable. Julie condones this action in typical FGBF fashion.

This is only the start of Lady Bird abandoning her best friend. When things don't work out with Danny (on account of him being gay), Lady Bird seeks to leave her sphere once again and glow up to what she desires to be; cool, popular and rich. She fixates this desire onto a boy of similar description, the pretension-made-flesh character of Kyle, expertly portrayed by Timothée Chalamet, and his friend Jenna, played by Odeya Rush.

Lady Bird approaches her relationship with Jenna strategically, hoping for an invitation into her friendship group and an opening to meet Kyle.

When in a class with Jenna, Lady Bird sits behind her and leans in as Jenna holds court telling a story. Julie comes and sits next to Lady Bird, offering her a packed lunch made by her mom's boyfriend, an established ritual that the two have (and another show of support and care that exists in Lady Bird's life), Lady Bird says, 'No thanks, I'm trying to lose weight'. The refusal of the packed lunch cuts off her connection to Julie as a part of her family, and the comment about weight is an indirect criticism of Julie's eating habits and reinforcement that thin equates to popularity.

Lady Bird establishes her friendship with Jenna by calling their teacher 'a cunt', language she hasn't used in the film up till this point. They then bond over graffitiing the teacher's car. This happens during the auditions for the school musical, somewhere Lady Bird wants to be but doesn't deem cool anymore. Julie goes without her, staying in her sphere without Lady Bird.

Of course, things don't work out for Lady Bird, and when she tries to justify her actions to Julie, Julie calls her on it. She screams, 'You can't do anything without being the centre of attention'. Julie, as the FGBF, fulfils her role of being an unwelcome mirror for the Thin Lead and is therefore ostracised so Lady Bird can go on to make more mistakes before realising she needs her friend.

When Lady Bird finally decides that she doesn't want to hang out with the horrible people she once idolised, she goes to find Julie on the night of prom. Julie is not dressed, crying on the couch. When Lady Bird asks why she is crying Julie says with heartbreaking honesty, 'Some people aren't built happy, you know?'

This level of character depth is rare for a FGBF. Julie admitting to being at the mercy of an inherent sadness, a pre-natural disposition to melancholy and depression, is real and honest and beautiful. Gerwig might have been making a comment here about just how oblivious Lady Bird is to the struggles of those around her, and about Julie's fortitude, but since Julie is not the main character and we are marching towards the end of the film, there is a hard cut between Julie crying in Lady Bird's arms, to them laughing and eating cookies in the kitchen, and Julie's problems melt away in the presence of her friend.

With the end of the story nigh and Lady Bird bound for college on the East Coast, I always wondered what happened to this sad girl with the biggest smile. Did Julie find contentment at the local community college? Did she find love? Did she and Lady Bird stay in touch or did she find friends who actually took the time to really know her? It's a shame that we as an audience never got the chance to.

It is sad that we were deprived of more time with Julie because Lady Bird sacrificed her friendship with her (depriving us of screen time with Julie) for a portion of the film, but the temporary breakdown of this female friendship is by no means the most tragic example of the FGBF being shafted by the Thin Lead's glow up.

Some FGBFs get *literally* sacrificed.

The Duffer Brothers' world-renowned show *Stranger Things* is revolutionary in its nostalgia mining, its aesthetic and its homage to the classic 80s action film and video game culture. As one of Netflix's flagship properties it has garnered record numbers of viewers on the service and is globally renowned and award winning.

As a viewer and fan myself I can attest to the show's excellent characterisation, acting, energy, design, soundtrack and so much more. It really is a favourite.

I just have one problem with it: the relationship between Nancy and Barb in Season One.

Nancy Wheeler, doe-eyed, studious teenager and big sister to one of the core four boys at the centre of the story. The first time we are introduced to Nancy, she is in her room, on her bed, on the phone to Barbara 'Barb' Holland. They are talking about a boy. Dustin, the sweetest and funniest of the core four, offers her the last slice of pizza and she slams the door in his face without answering him, cutting herself off from that group and their childhood friendship. Dustin even says, 'Your sister used to be cool' later to Mike.

Nancy's first character arc is trying to establish her boundaries with popular boy Steve Harrington, whom she has kissed a few times, ensuring she does not just become another notch on the bedpost to him while fighting her own sexual desires. She uses her need to study as her main defence against his charms, establishing her as both a good student and as someone at the beginning of her journey towards being sexually active.

Barb is Nancy's best friend. She appears in Episode 1 as Nancy walks into the High School and thus establishes her age. Barb sidles up to Nancy and her first line is, 'Did he call?' Immediately Barb is established to be Nancy's support person regarding her relationship. Their entire first conversation is all about Steve and Nancy; how many times they have kissed, how many times he called, whether she is planning to see him again. It is clear that Nancy is in new territory here and she is trying to convince her friend that things are not changing with her because of this new boy. Barb is unconvinced but supportive and gently mocking of Nancy's naivety.

Barb does not have a long arc within the show. In the second episode, Nancy is invited to come over to Steve's house since his parents are away. Nancy invites Barb and insists she comes too, saying, 'Well you can be like my guardian. Stop me from getting drunk and doing anything stupid'. Barb is the one to point out what

Nancy already knows; that the invitation primarily arose from the opportunity for Steve and Nancy to have sex for the first time. When Nancy denies this, Barb is the one to say, 'You are not this stupid'.

Nancy's refusal of the obvious and her playing dumb is the first sign of her shrugging off her qualities that are undesirable to the social hierarchy; her intelligence. She knows why she is there, and she knows that she wants to be there, she just brings Barb as a social ally and a means of leaving if things get too scary for her.

At the party, Nancy engages in activities that are not her usual, highlighted by Barb rolling her eyes over at the side of the party. Nancy shotguns a beer to the applause of Steve and his cronies, and when Nancy sees Barb judging her, she forces Barb to try it too. Even though Barb explicitly says, 'I don't want to', Nancy is the one to force her. When trying to puncture the can, Barb injures herself so must leave the group to take care of herself. This leaves Nancy with Steve and another couple, and seconds after Barb leaves, they all jump in the pool and kiss together. When they get out, Steve invites Nancy upstairs 'to change into dry clothes'.

As she ascends the stairs Barb comes back and tries to stop her. Barb says, 'This isn't you'. Fulfilling one of her main functions as a FGBF, Barb is the mirror Nancy doesn't want to look in. Nancy knows that she is kidding herself in following Steve up the stairs, she knows she is making important decisions based on whether she thinks Steve will approve, and she knows that Barb is the only one who can ruin the illusion she is spinning for herself through self-deception. As with Lady Bird and Julie, this is the breaking point for the friendship. Nancy tells Barb to go home without her and follows Steve up the stairs.

While Nancy is upstairs losing her virginity, Barb is attacked by a demon, dragged into 'The Upside Down' and killed, all the while screaming for Nancy to help her.

There is a trope in the horror genre called 'Death by Sex', which originates from an urban legend in the 50s. It basically dictates that any character in a horror movie who has sex is almost immediately seen to die. Think of Paris Hilton running around a warehouse screaming in the 00s reboot *House of Wax*. She has sex in a tent and immediately after her sexual partner is stabbed in the neck and she is hunted down and killed.

Sex on screen is a rare thing because of the importance of protecting audiences and the need to maintain a line between cinema and porn. While many on-screen stories need to insinuate sex and a sexual relationship between characters without ever actually depicting sex on screen, the kiss has been accepted over time to depict and connotate sex in screen-based stories.

While audiences widely accept an adult, consenting, heteronormative kiss on screen to have connotations of sex, it then makes characters having sex seem extreme and leans into the tired assumption that women who have sex on screen are whores.

The opposite of 'Death by Sex' is 'The Final Girl', in which the chaste, sensible and reserved female character is most likely the one to survive the ordeal of the horror, while all her friends have died along the way (most likely through 'Death by Sex'). The original 'Final Girl' was Jamie Lee Curtis' portrayal of Laurie in John Carpenter's *Halloween* franchise. While horror is the only genre in film and television where women get more screen time and speaking parts than men (as researched by the Geena Davis Institute on Gender in Media), these tropes are rooted in sexism, where any woman who has sex is seen as 'the whore' and, therefore, doomed to die.

Stranger Things has always toed the line between sci-fi and horror and has done wonderful things to revive the 80s action and adventure genre, and while the inversion of this trope could be seen as a positive thing, it also has horrible connotations for the FGBF.

If The Final Girl trope was followed traditionally, it would be Nancy and Steve who were killed off by the creature and Barb would have emerged victorious from the trials.

Nancy does come into her own throughout the series; the trials of Season One reveal her to be the bravest and most savvy of the brilliant ensemble cast. She takes up weapons, goes hunting for the beasts and becomes the show's own take on 'The Final Girl'. This is amazing to see, but did Barb really have to be literally sacrificed for this to happen?

After the show's airing there was such an outcry about the fate of Barb that the hashtag #JusticeforBarb trended globally. Barb, as a character, never had any onus of her own, she was there purely to be Nancy's true mirror, reflecting the sacrifices she was making of her own person all in pursuit of a boy and being part of the popular crowd. Her only purpose was to die in order for Nancy to get some perspective on her actions.

The strength of *Stranger Things* comes from its ensemble cast, having a ragtag group of plucky people pull together to save their less than ordinary town and the people in it. *Was there no space in this group for Barb?*

At the time of writing, *Stranger Things* has aired four seasons and has a fifth and final season in production. The cast, lore and dangers have all grown exponentially, yet strangely, in all that time very few named characters have actually died. Apart from Barb, the only other high-profile deaths have been Bob and Billy. Billy in Season Three has a 'Villain to Hero' redemption arc but the death of Bob in Season Two, portrayed by the legendary Sean Astin, was a hard one to swallow.

First appearing in Season Two as Joyce's new boyfriend, plus size Bob, manager of a small tech store in Hawkins, is presented as boring and mundane with an insufferable positivity about him. Those qualities, and the fact that he is just genuinely a brilliant, brave and wonderful guy, end up being exactly what is needed when things get hairy in the Hawkins Laboratory. While he helps everyone inside escape, before he can himself, he is killed by Devil Dogs in a brutal attack.

With the only fat members of the cast being killed, it makes me wonder if being thin is a required necessity to deal with all the horrors of Hawkins and be part of the *Stranger Things* ensemble cast? While Bob has more time on screen and more episodes than Barb ever did, he still died when encountering the otherworld creatures for the first time, just like Barb, even though many other characters faced them and escaped more than once.

The flipping of The Final Girl and the Death by Sex tropes in Season One can be seen as a clever inverting of two tired tropes that plague the horror genre but for me this, apparently progressive, narrative move is nullified by the fact that the creators of the show decided to kill off the FGBF because she has fulfilled her purpose within two episodes.

Barb was a fan favourite and could have been so much more. I think the creators must have realised the mistakes of Season One and took a course of correction. As the seasons of *Stranger Things* go on a huge effort is made to champion female friendship, firstly with Max and Elle in Season Three and then with Nancy and Robin in Season Four. With Nancy growing into a gun-toting, unflinchingly badass heroine, it makes me wonder just how much more she could have been with her best friend by her side.

I don't wonder what Barb could have been because I have absolutely no basis on which to base my assumptions. The wants, needs, loves, hates and traits of Barb were never given a single minute of screen time and that, for me, is the biggest tragedy. Without that, we will never have #JusticeforBarb.

To have a truly progressive portrayal of the fat girl character in High School, would the creators have to spend too much time unpicking the cinematic language and the well-established tropes? Would it be too difficult to tell an interesting story while ensuring audiences don't see the fat girl in a school uniform and automatically make assumptions based on the hundreds of films and episodes of television they have seen before? *Stranger Things* is breaking the mould in so many ways already, it's a shame this isn't one of them.

The need for teenagers to reinvent themselves is a subject explored often in film and television, but there needs to be an acknowledgement that there is room for the character to grow and learn something fundamental about themselves in this transformation. We know Nancy and Lady Bird learned a lot about themselves but Julie and Barb were not given the chance to.

What if the fat girl was not the best friend in a High School drama, but the lead character? Would that make a difference?

• • •

THE CYRANO DE BERGERAC EFFECT

In my final year of school, I studied French at Higher. I wasn't very good at it, but I enjoyed the class, and my teacher was absolutely bonkers, which was always amusing. She had all these off-the-wall teaching techniques like making up rap songs to help us memorise our verbs (which never worked), but not all her ideas were daft. She would show us films in French without the subtitles to throw us into the language, which as a film buff I found really useful.

It was in her class that I was first introduced to the 1990 Jean-Paul Rappeneau film *Cyrano de Bergerac*, an adaptation of the 1890s Edmond Rostand play. The lead character, Cyrano, is a famous swordsman and poet, acclaimed by the men in his regiment and his town for being quick with the sword and quicker with his wit. Despite being beloved by all, Cyrano has no self-confidence when it comes to love, as he was born with a comically large nose.

In the story, Cyrano is in love with Roxanne but can never tell her how he feels. He is so sure that she can never love him or be attracted to him because of his nose. So, when a young and hand-some soldier, Christian, joins his regiment and catches the eye of Roxanne, Cyrano sees an opportunity. Christian has no way with words, so Cyrano helps him write beautiful love letters to Roxanne, knowing it will be the only way he will ever be able to tell Roxanne how he really feels.

I was absolutely obsessed with this film. It was dramatic, romantic and incredibly written, and the performance from Gerard Depardieu was something I had never seen before; he was tortured and humble and shy as well as outrageous and whippet quick. Cyrano is a tragic character in that he could never fathom a world in which Roxanne could ever love him back, so he hides behind Christian, but it's clear that Roxanne falls in love with Cyrano's words, not Christian's looks.

No matter how many times I watched the film, I hoped the story would magically change and Cyrano find the courage to say what he felt and put himself out there.

The story of Cyrano has been adapted many times; more recently with the 1987 Fred Schepisi film *Roxanne* starring Steve Martin and

Daryl Hannah, the 2021 Joe Wright original musical film *Cyrano* starring Peter Dinklage, and the National Theatre's updated verse play *Cyrano* by Edmond Rostand and Martin Crimp, starring James McAvoy.

After the whole #JusticeforBarb fiasco, Netflix realised it had missed an opportunity to place an actor with so much public admiration – one who became a fan favourite even though they were killed off after two episodes – front and centre in one of their properties.

Almost exactly two years later, Netflix released *Sierra Burgess is a Loser*, directed by Ian Samuels and starring Shannon Purser (Barb) as the title character, Sierra.

The story is a supposed modern retelling of *Cyrano de Bergerac*, a claim I have very strong qualms about. Liberties were, understandably, taken when gender swapping the roles for the adaptation, however a lot of these liberties led to characteristics and plot devices that have seriously negative and dangerous connotations. There are some important choices that are worth comparing and questioning, as they reinforce a very different and skewed reading of the original story. Firstly, the way the adaptation interpreted the central character's 'big nose' portrayal and secondly, the contemporary retelling of the deception of Roxanne.

Sierra Burgess is in her senior year of High School. She is smart and dedicated, determined to get into the college of her dreams. She is not very popular but she has very supportive and loving parents and has a close relationship with her best friend, Dan.

The film opens with Sierra getting out of the shower in the morning. We see close-ups of various parts of her plus size, towel-wrapped body, before she wipes steam from the mirror to reveal her gorgeous, fresh face. She stares at her reflection and mutters, 'You are a magnificent beast', before throwing herself a dazzling smile. When I first watched this film, this opening filled me with so much hope. Sure, they were going in a bit heavy-handed with the HD close-ups of her body before ever getting to her face, but the unfiltered and unflinching approach to this central character gave me hope that I might be in for a lovely time.

Fuck was I disappointed. I waited for the reveal of what would be her 'big nose' moment as a modern-day Cyrano – maybe she is grumpy or overly cocky or just really terrible at public speaking – but nothing came. She is smart and offers a tutoring service, she is witty with her parents and 'doesn't obsess over looks' in an unhealthy manner. She seems to be a perfectly well-adjusted teenager.

I realised then that the film didn't pull its punches. Her getting out of the shower *was* the reveal. Sierra's 'big nose', the thing that makes her see herself as completely unlovable, is her body.

When Sierra's core want is revealed (to go to Stanford) at a meeting with her guidance counsellor, she is asked about her extra-curricular activities that will make her stand out for college admissions boards. She has none, except tutoring. Sierra is a completely normal student. She gets good grades, knows how to stand up for herself against Veronica's (the adaptation's 'Christian' character and High School Queen Bee) insults, and seems to get through her day without any huge struggle. And yet, despite all this normalness, she is still a loser. An outcast. Why?

In the original *Cyrano de Bergerac*, Cyrano was neither of these things; he was beloved by all. His core deception, by which I mean the one thing that everyone including the audience knows but he doesn't until the end, is that his big nose has no impact on how worthy and deserving he is of love.

For most heroes in fiction, their narrative journey involves confronting and overcoming their core deception; the same is true for Sierra. However, comparing her slightly plus size body to the comically and grotesquely large nose of Cyrano is dangerous.

The nose, written as a 'deformity' (which as a term is a stretch, as having a small nose is really only a thing to be praised in Western beauty standards), is in itself-problematic, but it was written in a time far before the wisdom of today where it is understood to be wrong to ostracise and alienate people for things they cannot control such as the appearance of their face. However, in each screen adaptation since the original text a prosthetic has been used to take the nose from the world of rather unfortunate genetics to the fantastical, comedic and unbelievable. It is meant to be so outlandish that it could not possibly exist in the real world, which makes Cyrano's hatred of it more understandable when we see it.

For Sierra's size to truly be comparable to Cyrano's big nose, it would have to be something that she hated about herself. Something that in her eyes was the unavoidable object in the way of her desires. Her size, and her belief that it made her unworthy of romantic love, would have to be presented by the creators as her core deception. Something that everyone, including the audience, knew not to be true.

This is not how it went down in *Sierra Burgess is a Loser*.

Sierra is a confident and capable young woman, able to love her body despite the world. Sierra's size is not something she believes to be an obstacle. If it was, it would be her core deception. Because Sierra does not see herself and her body as problematic when she steps out of the shower at the start of the film, her size as a barrier between her and romantic love is being presented by the creators as a *universal truth*.

As the audience, we are meant to see Sierra and – despite her assurance that she is happy with her body and herself – to understand that she *cannot* find love. She is in High School and is fat, so unlovable. The genre dictates it.

There is no prosthetic used here, no fat suit or anything to take her body out of the world of rather unfortunate genetics and into the world of the fantastical, comedic and unbelievable, there is just this young woman (who is hovering on the line of plus size) and her perfectly normal body, and the understanding that we should easily draw comparison between this and Cyrano's nose.

I don't understand how the creators of this story could ever hope to make a piece that is faithful, kind and progressive in any way (as it had a chance to be by making courageous decisions such as gender swapping the lead role) when *this* is the universal truth being presented. Sierra no longer has to go on a journey within herself, she has to fight the system that is High School.

In *Sierra Burgess is a Loser* the character of Roxanne is substituted by a nerdy but handsome football player from a neighbouring school, Jayme, played by king of Netflix teen rom-com Noah Centineo. In the modern age, when writing love letters is not really in the language of the modern teenager, there is so much room to play with the adaptation of the deception of Roxanne, or in this case Jayme.

When Jayme approaches Veronica to ask for her number, Veronica gives him Sierra's number as a joke, deeming him to be a loser because his friends *look* like losers. Once again, the creators are taking progressive characters and actively running in the opposite direction of their positive attributes to reinforce cruel and outdated stereotypes. Jayme texts Sierra thinking she is Veronica, and the two begin to chat. When Sierra realises that Jayme thinks he is texting Veronica, she is torn. She carries on chatting to him, thinking it will be harmless, but when she starts to like him, and Jayme professes to like her (who he believes to be Veronica) Sierra justifies her actions because she believes that Jayme has fallen for *her* through their communication via phone and texts.

Substituting love letters for text messages makes perfect sense in the contemporary setting of this adaptation, and while the interchange between Sierra and Jayme is full of red flags, such as Jayme sending her unsolicited topless photos and Sierra deliberately being vague with her responses, this is glossed over as a structural necessity to move the story forward in a way that embodies the spirit of the original story. However, *Sierra Burgess is a Loser* is so far removed from *Cyrano de Bergerac* that all the problematic elements that somehow keep getting worse as the story progresses can only be laid at the feet of the creators. Their choices have dangerous and damaging connotations, and the fact that they present these narrative choices as a romance storyline is quite frankly inexcusable.

If this was an honest adaptation, then Sierra and Jayme would have been friends already. Veronica would have felt the same way for Jayme as he did for her. Sierra's words would have only helped benefit a love that already existed, giving words to Veronica's true but indescribable feelings, aiding in and facilitating the happiness of two beloved people in her life.

As it's not, Sierra straight up catfishes Jayme by pretending to be someone she is not and continuing in the ruse beyond the point where she figured out how he got her number in the first place.

The plot gets even more convoluted when Jayme gets impatient with only communicating over calls and texts and wants to have a meet up. Sierra somehow manages to recruit the help of Veronica, who agrees to be part of the deception and becomes friends with Sierra in the process. Their first real bonding experience is when they video call Jayme with Veronica in front of the camera and Sierra behind it, Veronica miming along to Sierra's words and claiming there is a delay on the feed. After Veronica agrees to go on a date with Jayme, and when Jayme wants to kiss her at the end of the night, she tells him to close his eyes and swaps herself out so Sierra can kiss him.

This is an act of sexual assault. Jayme did not consent to kissing Sierra. At this point in the film he still has no idea that Sierra even exists. To present this narrative as romantic is negligent and dangerous. If you follow this justification through to the end or accept that kissing is the cinematic language for sex, the filmmakers are condoning rape by deception with this narrative.

What's more, it is presenting Sierra's kiss with Jayme as the only way this could possibly happen for the two of them. That plus size girls in High School can only ever have romantic love if it is sought through deception and taken without consent.

This turn in the story was enough to make me want to turn it off entirely, something I never do, but I was morbidly intrigued as to how the filmmakers would try and justify this action, reconcile the truth between Sierra and Jayme and ultimately get to the happy ending, which I knew was coming because happy endings always happen in the Netflix original High School genre.

Jayme sees Veronica again and goes in for a kiss (which is under-standable since he believes that they have already kissed) but Veronica pulls away, not wanting to betray Sierra. Sierra sees this kiss, and in retribution she releases to the whole school a private photo of Veronica that her ex took of her unknowingly.

Catfishing. Sexual assault by deception. Revenge porn. This film really pulls out all the stops.

31

When Sierra is discovered by Jayme as a catfish, he tells her to stay away from him, and Sierra goes home in floods. When her parents ask her what is wrong, she cries, 'It's easy for you to spout your self-esteem BS, but do you have any idea what it's like to be a teenage girl and to look like this?'

This is so different from the girl at the start of the film, standing and smiling at herself in the mirror and declaring self-love. Is a teenage boy fancying a head cheerleader instead of her all it takes for that to fall apart? Is her self-love at the start of the film revealed to be entirely superficial, naive and completely hollow in the face of the real world? The creators here reinforce a world where all fat women must feel insecure about their weight.

So, according to Sierra, no amount of love, support, friendship and encouragement can ever be enough to negate the societal hatred of plus size women. There's nothing that anyone can do that can stop the cruelty, raise the confidence or make space for plus size women and girls to just be themselves in their day-to-day lives.

Quite frankly, how fucking dare she.

Even after all the horrible things she did, Jayme still forgives Sierra, and they share a (consensual) kiss before the homecoming dance. When he confronts her about the wrongness of her actions, she asks him, 'Do you ever feel like the world is conspiring against you to tell you you're not good enough?'

Yes. Of course we do. The world is conspiring to tell plus size women and girls that they are not good enough, and a huge perpetrator of that is the mainstream media. But this doesn't in any way excuse her behaviour and the actions she chose to take in the film.

The constant rehashing of existing stereotypes in the YA and High School genre of film and television, leaning into these tropes in ways that justify the negative treatment of plus size young women, has severe consequences for those young women in the real world.

Being a teenage girl is hell! Just getting through the hormone changes, body development and the revolving door of menstruating issues is hard enough without school. It is even harder for plus size girls. Imagine trying to get through an already challenging time in your life surrounded by people that you have literally no escape from, that you have no control over, and who are fed the same narrative year after year that you, because of your larger body, are not worthy of basic human compassion.

And the infuriating thing is, *it doesn't have to be this way.*

Creators of film and television have literally all the power to present stories in worlds that are kind and progressive, but they choose not to. While it is a given that High School is an established social environment where plus sized people are treated unfairly leaning into this trope is a choice made by the creators.

If the creators decided to simply present a world in which this blatant fatphobia in schools did not exist, the audiences would believe it and still follow the story, trusting that the storytellers know what they are doing.

An example of this in a different context is Eugene and Dan Levy's Canadian family sitcom, *Schitt's Creek*.

A rich family loses all their money and are forced to move to Schitt's Creek, a worthless backwater town in the middle of nowhere, where they have to pick up the pieces of their lives surrounded by the support of the colourful (if uncultured) locals.

A huge part of the development of the central characters lies in queer narratives. Dan Levy's character, David, for example, is openly pansexual and hopeless in love. While it would have been so easy to lean into the stereotype of small-town rural America being a hotbed of homophobia and racism, the show exists in a world without either. The concept simply does not exist.

In a beautiful and touching scene, where David's dad, Johnny, accidentally outs his son's partner, Patrick, to their parents, David goes to attempt to smooth things over. In the room with his boyfriend's parents, Patrick's dad is visibly upset and asks, 'Is it something we did, David?' David assumes that this hurt comes from having a gay son, and in thinking that Patrick's queerness was somehow 'caused' by nurture instead of nature. When David tries to assure them that Patrick is still the same person they have always known and loved, Patrick's mother cuts off this thought with a firm, 'David, we're not upset that Patrick is gay'.

David holds his breath, looks to Patrick's dad for confirmation and is met with utter acceptance. The upset comes from feeling like they failed as parents, because for some reason Patrick felt he had to hide that he was in a significant relationship. When David realises this, and that he doesn't have to stand in the face of homophobia to protect his partner from harm, all the wind is knocked out of him.

Breathily, he says, 'Okay, for a moment there I thought this was going to get very dark' and wipes away a tear.

The beautiful thing about *Schitt's Creek* is that it never ever gets very dark.

Instead of getting on their soapbox and making a big to-do about how bad society is and how damaging it is to queer people, they show just how easy it is to have a world without any space for bigotry.

This is something that can easily be done with fatphobia.

It is easy to believe when seeing the negative treatment of plus size women on our screens that it is necessary, that it is essential to the story to ground the world in realism, but *every time* it is an artistic choice made by the writer, the director or the producer.

It is understandable that works grounded in realism should in some way reflect both the positive and the negative attitudes of the world they occupy, but why should art rooted in absurdism, romanticism and expressionism use these tropes when they aren't bound by being realistic?

In the Netflix television show *Bridgerton*, an adaptation of a series of Regency era romantic novels (or 'gusset-busters' as I like to call them – I have *many* shelves stacked with books such as these) the wonderful creators at Shondaland, the company run by Shonda Rhimes, made a small but massively impactful change in their adaptation; they made Queen Charlotte a black woman. As such, the Ton (the period name for High Society London) is a wonderfully diverse place. This is amazing! Nonetheless, introducing Penelope Featherington (played by plus size actor Nicola Coughlan) on screen with a comment from her sister within seconds saying,

'She's two stone heavier than she ought to be' is not so amazing.

These choices have ramifications.

My teenage years were when I first discovered my love of film and television and I set my sights on one day being in those decision-making roles. My teenage years were also the time of my sexual and romantic awakenings, and my first awareness of my own body.

I can still quote *Twilight* from memory. I can still hear my heart racing the first time I saw Katniss and Peeta reach for the berries, and I still remember the feeling of guilt when America Fererra pointed to her beautiful hips and referred to herself as 'all this' in *The Sisterhood of Travelling Pants*. These stories stayed with me, they are still with me and they shaped a lot of my interests and hobbies and pursuits growing up. They had a direct impact on my life.

Society told me to hate myself, and I did. It told me I wasn't important and I believed it. I resented that I was not like most other girls in my friendship group, that I couldn't buy my bras from Primark, couldn't participate in PE without being leered at for something outwith my control, couldn't ever be with a boy without feeling like it was all part of a cruel prank and that boys couldn't possibly like me when I looked like I did.

It took a long time to undo that damage. A long time to unpick the learnings from my brain and my sense of self. I can't think about how much time and energy I had to spend convincing myself that I was not, in fact, ugly, lazy, disposable and lesser without getting really angry.

And while it would be easy to say, 'The 90s and 00s were another time, things have gotten much better since then', all the examples I have mentioned in this chapter were released within the last five years.

It kills me to think there are still teenage girls going through the same things I went through in High School, the same social torture and judgment for their bodies, who look to their screens for comfort and for assurance that the worst that people throw at them is simply not true, to only be met with Julie, Barb and Sierra.

These stories wrap around your heart and stay with you forever. We should be doing so much more than we are to make sure our girls aren't carrying hateful thoughts about themselves well into their adult lives.

Enough is not being done for the YA genre, for the industry or for the teenage girls in our audience.

CHAPTER 4

'Laughing at' or 'Laughing with'

One thing I learned early in life, something that actually made my time in High School somewhat bearable, is that comedy is currency.

If you can make the people around you laugh, you are safe, for a time. If you make them laugh, they are laughing *with* you, not *at* you.

Being brought up in Glasgow, in a working-class family and community, I come from a long line of funny people. I might be the first person in my family to have made a career out of being funny, but I am the least funny person in my family. That's not me being self-deprecating, I'm just acknowledging the timing, rhythm and artistry that goes into the inherent storytelling talent of my father, my granny and my aunts.

I was raised on their stories. I was raised on the stories of Billy Connolly. I was raised on the stories of hardship and struggle, of my granny sleeping in one bed with six siblings and being sent away during the evacuation and made to climb up and clean the inside of chimneys. Despite their essential tragedy, whenever she would tell me these stories from her past she would have me in tears of laughter every time. My granny told me many things but one thing really stuck with me, 'If you don't laugh you'll greet'.

This basically means that if you don't laugh about the world and the hardships and the terrible things that happen every day, you'll be crushed under the despair of it. Laughing is how we deal with the problems and make them that bit easier to manage. My granny is a woman who managed and I think, because of this, I can remember being culturally aware of the power of other funny women, even if they were before my time. Women like Dawn French, Jo Brand, Victoria Wood, Julie Walters and Catherine Tate, all women who broke through the boys' club of the BBC to be unapologetically funny and, more importantly, unapologetically honest.

When I was young, I had an overcrowded mouth that led to me having seven teeth removed including one of my front teeth. (Yes,

I had three front teeth, it was really something.) I also had glasses and stringy brown hair. I was a cute toddler, but once the baby teeth were gone so was any hope that I might turn out conventionally beautiful. It was at this time that I remember an aunt commenting to my mother, 'She's no looker but at least she's smart and funny'.

I took that and I ran with it.

I have always been a people pleaser and an overachiever, so when I realised that the key to my success was through academic achievement and my ability to make people laugh, my whole life became about those two things.

As I got closer to the end of my High School career and it was clear that I was bound for a career in the arts and, much to the dismay of my father, I said goodbye to any studies of maths and sciences. Sensing I could make people laugh through creative mediums, I let my need for academic excellence fall by the wayside. This might have had something to do with the fact that my sister was such a natural genius at maths and sciences I could never compete with her, even though she was five years younger than me. She was doing my algebra homework when she was seven.

I knew I'd have to stand out in other ways. I threw myself into telling stories, and I knew I had to make them funny.

Being fat and funny is a complicated relationship. While, like I've said, it's an easy way to prove your worth to any social group by providing levity and general good vibes, it also places you closer to the situations that open you up to being ridiculed for your size.

We live in a society where being fat is an offence punishable by mockery, so when you are a self-proclaimed fat and funny person people are expecting you to make the most obvious joke; one at your own expense.

This causes me to ask the most important question. *When you tell a joke, are the people around you laughing at you or laughing with you?*

If they're laughing *with* you then you are a part of the collective joy. If they're laughing *at* you then you are on the outside of their enjoyment, standing apart as an object to be mocked from a distance.

You would think it's easy to tell the difference since the two are so contrary. Since the negative treatment of fat people, however, is so ingrained in our collective social consciousness, it's not always obvious that mistreatment is happening. Laughing at and laughing with are so often interchangeable, and it is because of this that so many negative representations of fat people, especially women, have been continually trotted out in film and television for decades.

It is important to be able to critically examine these jokes made around, in the presence of, or by plus size women in film and television. If we were able to tell the difference every time between laughing at and laughing with, then we would be more empowered to call out bullying when we see it.

From what I can tell there are two mechanisms in film and television that masquerade as a positive and inclusive representation of fat women, but really are just clever and subtle forms of mockery. The first mechanism is the use of self-deprecation *by* fat women characters. The second is equating confidence with insanity.

I mentioned previously being aware of Jo Brand. Her soft monotone and cutting observations had me in stitches. I remember seeing a televised section of her stand up when I was quite young. I can't remember the wider context of the show, how long it was or where I was when I saw it, but there's this one bit that still sticks out crystal clear in my memory.

After her introduction, Jo started a new story involving her husband and her daughters. She then stopped in order to address a silent concern she assumed the audience was having. She said something along the lines of, 'That's right, someone actually wanted to shag this'. She made herself the butt of the joke. She felt that to get the audience to go along with her story, one in which she was happily married to a man, she actually had to stop to acknowledge that it's hard to believe that any normal man would want to marry a woman like her. Like she needed to address that assumption to keep the audience on side for the rest of her story.

This self-deprecating attitude can be received as progressive – it's her body, she can talk about it in whatever way she wants – however, when she stands in front of a room full of people who have paid to see her and speaks about herself negatively in order to make people laugh and connect to her, I take from it that she has made a choice to offer herself up as comedic fodder in order to be socially acceptable, and that I should do the same.

It doesn't make a difference whether Jo Brand believed she had to get the obvious joke out of the way first by mocking herself or whether she genuinely thought she would create a greater rapport with her audience by giving them permission to laugh at her fatness. She still degraded herself for the pleasure of others because it was what she was expected to do.

I remember that. Being expected to. I remember in school when speaking to the scary kids in my year when we were placed in groups together or forced to sit next to each other in class. They didn't like me and I didn't like them but they had the power and I knew it. I knew that they were only ever seconds away from using the forced proximity to eviscerate me for my fatness, and I knew that I had to be smart and funny to survive. It's always been how I survived. One of the easiest ways for me to do that was to make fun of myself. Make them laugh. Make out that I knew that my body was a mockable offence and I was just as disgusted as everyone else was. That I knew my place and was more than okay with it. By laughing at myself I gave the others permission to do the same, but when they did it was without the poison sting of malicious bullying. It was a gentler kind of mocking, one with slightly more camaraderie. I was still being laughed at, but I was laughing too, so it was a little easier.

I unlearned that lesson slowly over time. I unlearned the assumption that I should be the first person to give others permission to laugh at me. It took a long time to give up self-deprecation in favour of self-championing, and while it's a harder path to follow, it's definitely better for me and my self-worth.

Jo Brand is a patron of the Funny Women Awards, an organisation dedicated to celebrating, promoting and championing women working in the comedy stage and screen industries in the UK, and the work she does to lift other funny women up, myself included, knows no bounds. I often think about that set, those words and I cannot align them with the powerful, funny woman I know to be working so hard behind the scenes. I wonder whether it is all just an act, a way to survive, or whether Jo is still doing the unlearning I did too. I hope she is, because she is nothing short of sexy.

Speaking of sexy, this brings me onto the second mechanism masquerading as progressive representation of fat women on screen. It is a much more subtle and, in my opinion, sinister way of writing fat characters. It's the equivalent of Regina George saying, 'Oh my God, I love your skirt, where did you get it?' to your face and calling it ugly behind your back. After all, how can you say that a confident and sexually empowered woman on screen is a negative and damaging representation of fat women?

By making 'confidence' synonymous with 'insane' in these characters.

REBEL WILSON AND FAT AMY

Pitch Perfect is a 2012 musical comedy written by Kay Cannon, directed by Elizabeth Banks and Jason Moore, that follows an all-female collegiate a cappella group, the Barden Bellas, in the quest for the national championship. While the film stars a stellar ensemble cast, the plot of the film mainly follows Thin Lead Beca, played by Anna Kendrick – an outcast with dreams of becoming a music producer – breaking down her tough barriers and learning to accept the bonds of female friendship. Her and a bunch of other misfits join the Bellas and together they shrug off the stifled traditions of the group to make a more progressive and inclusive group with a more appealing sound.

Also a newbie to the Bellas, and soon to be best friend to Beca, is the Australian wildcard FGBF, Fat Amy, played by Rebel Wilson.

Now, I get that Fat Amy isn't your average FGBF, and on the surface she seems to tick every progressive box there is. She's smart, funny and sexy and she is this while reclaiming the insult of 'fat' in her name. I love the idea of a character proudly reclaiming the word for her own confidence; Fat Amy, however, does specify that she does so in order to prevent the 'twig bitches' of the world doing it for her. She is not doing so in celebration, but in self-defence.

Fat Amy's character is exceedingly difficult to prove as a negative representation of fat women in film because everything she says and does seems to be refreshing and unapologetic, which is great. Nonetheless, as I mentioned earlier, the mechanics of equating confidence with insanity is a very subtle way to laugh at a comedy character rather than with her. Fat Amy is a zany addition to the *Pitch Perfect* ensemble cast and she always keeps the Thin Lead on her toes, but her off-the-wall characteristics make it hard to really relate to her as a person. Her ideas are so eccentric that we, the audience, don't ever really know what she's thinking or feeling, which alienates her from us and makes her more of a thing than a person. Her eccentric tendencies show her to live outside the conventions of society, we must assume that she is so unaware or unable to process her place in the social hierarchy as a fat woman surrounded by Thin Leads. Therefore, her confidence in the face of a fatphobic and unkind society are suddenly called into question.

Is Fat Amy a smart, confident, funny and sexy queen who doesn't care what anyone thinks about her, or is she just plain 'crazy'?

The first time we meet Fat Amy is when Chloe and Aubrey, two seniors and the only remaining members of the Bellas after the previous class's graduation, are recruiting new members at a sign-up stall. Aubrey has high expectations for women with both perfect pitch and 'bikini ready bodies', whatever that means, but Chloe pushes to just look for good singers. Fat Amy happens to be walking by, hears this and shows an interest in joining. She shows off her vocal talents by being able to sing and match pitch, but also demonstrates a talent she holds in high esteem, 'mermaid dancing'. This is basically just her lying on the floor wiggling slightly as if her legs have been tied together.

Straight away, Fat Amy is not only shown to be slightly physically inept, but also deluded, as this is her idea of a professional level of dancing. We, the audience, wonder what else is she deluded about?

Throughout the film she is shown to be physically inept over and over again, even to the point where she comes across as a bad singer when she belts her audition of Kelly Clarkson's 'Since U Been Gone' so enthusiastically it reads as out of tune, only moments after she proved she *could* sing at the sign-up stall. In the first rehearsal she says she doesn't want to do any cardio work, and when all the other girls are running laps around the auditorium, Fat Amy is lying on her side on a row of chairs claiming that she is practising a kind of exercise called 'horizontal running'.

Fat Amy is also, in places, suggested to be a pathological liar. She makes strange and impossible claims such as, 'I've wrestled dingoes and crocodiles simultaneously' and admits to her real name being 'Fat Patricia'. These lies are so outlandish yet deep rooted, it makes the audience doubt everything that Fat Amy says and makes them think she is 'crazy'. Because of this when she makes her claims of being confident within herself, her body and her sexuality, the audience disregard them and assume she is lying, deluded, or both. They don't have to face up to the unfathomability of a fat woman being confident in herself, because Fat Amy, for whatever reason, doesn't count.

This isn't unique. In Amy Schumer's 2018 movie *I Feel Pretty*, it takes a literal head injury in order for her to see herself as beautiful. Schumer's many criticisms of herself include her weight, even though she is not plus size (she is just not entertainment thin). Again, the creators are suggesting that in order for a plus size woman to find herself attractive she must exist in an altered or 'abnormal' mental state.

I love to see a plus size woman on screen in touch with her sexuality, it's delightfully refreshing, and I am sure the creators portrayed Fat Amy that way in the hopes of her coming off as different from your average FGBF. She talks to men easily and confesses that she joined the Bellas because she wanted to hang out with really cool women and because she was getting tired of all her boyfriends. Not only does this show that Fat Amy is sexually active and empowered but she is the object of sexual desire by many men. The fact that *she* is the character being pursued by many men subverts the trope of the Blonde Bombshell. While I can appreciate the subversion of this trope, it does make Fat Amy the punchline. The comedy is meant to be derived from the 'surprise' that Fat Amy has multiple lovers vying for her attention; surprise shown by the other thin female characters in the group and by the audience, unintentionally underlining the creators' assumptions that fat women are not a 'normal' object of desire.

Fat Amy does have a romantic arc over the course of *Pitch Perfect* (and its sequel), in the form of the arrogant and awful (plus size)

Bumper, the overconfident leader of the group that is the Bellas' main competition, The Treblemakers. When Bumper first meets Fat Amy he tells her to her face that she is the most disgusting person he has ever seen, and then asks her if they should kiss. Bumper targets Amy, not because he is attracted to her but because he perceives her to be the easiest target, assuming she has low self-esteem so will be amenable to his attention. Amy likens the thought of kissing him to the thought of doing crystal meth, which I found hilarious, but the smackdown is short-lived as the pair are perceived to be hooking up over the first film and then develop a relationship in the sequel. (*Bingo!* Fat women only hooking up with fat men.)

I found this relationship formalising in the sequel to be odd, seeing as how beloved Fat Amy was by fans around the world. Surely we all think that Fat Amy deserves better than Bumper, right?

Pitch Perfect was an instant success, with wonderful music, a strong female friendship dynamic and a FGBF character that was a gift to meme culture. Fat Amy's one-liners and unique views along with Wilson's off the wall performance launched her career as a plus size comedy actress.

Wilson, in interviews, actually equated her success in comedy to her gaining weight. She believed that when she was thinner her co-stars who lived in bigger bodies got bigger laughs on stage, and it made her want to gain weight to be laughed at more. I personally believe it's a very naive way of thinking and also quite reductive to position thinness and fatness being so easy a choice, but the star's delight in being in a bigger body and counting it as a contributing factor in her success can only be seen as a positive.

Pitch Perfect tries so hard to break the FGBF tropes but, like with many stories that try to do the same, the attempt to break the tropes only ended up in furthering them. While Fat Amy is hilarious, at no point are you laughing with her as she is never trying to make you laugh. Her one-liners are played straight, her eccentric personality borders on unhinged and her exaggerated sexuality is aggressive, and whenever there is a hint of her being a progressive character, such as the mentioning of her many boyfriends, we are reminded that she is a pathological liar.

What I got from *Pitch Perfect* is this: the only reason that a fat woman can have genuine confidence, self-assurance and sexual liberation is if they are so far removed from awareness of societal norms and culture, that they fall under the damaging umbrella term of 'crazy'. The creators of *Pitch Perfect* are saying that Fat Amy couldn't possibly find herself attractive if she had a sound mind.

This is still 'laughing at'.

While Wilson has benefited from this role, going on to play many other roles in films such as *Isn't It Romantic*, *Jojo Rabbit*, *How to be Single* and *Cats*, she is yet to portray anything that deviates from this detached from reality persona she crafted so perfectly in *Pitch Perfect*. I have absolutely no issues with Wilson as an actor, she is so popular because she is so good at what she does, but I have serious qualms with the roles she continuously plays. While the characters may be different, the tropes are the same. So much so that looking at Wilson's career, you would assume that there is no deviating away from the 'laughing at' mechanism.

Thankfully, I believe there *are* examples of 'laughing with'; examples of plus size women in comedy that are fully-fledged characters without being the butt of the joke.

MELISSA McCARTHY AND SOOKIE ST. JAMES

I don't know whether this makes me just another nostalgic millennial or a Basic Bitch, but every time Autumn comes around I get a hankering for a *Gilmore Girls* rewatch.

This late 90s to early 00s series created by Amy Sherman-Palladino centres around mother, Lorelai, and daughter, also called Lorelai (Rory for short), as they navigate life, love and growth in the small town of Stars Hollow, Connecticut. Because the two are close in age (Lorelai had Rory when she was sixteen), the pair have a unique mother-daughter relationship that is refreshing.

Lorelai is the manager of an inn and works alongside her best friend, Sookie St. James, the haphazard, clumsy, yet permanently delightful head chef. It is established in Episode 1 that the pair want to one day open their own inn as equal partners, which is made clear after Sookie causes a calamity in the kitchen and Lorelai has to remind her friend that she needs to stay alive for that dream to become a reality.

Sookie is a fat woman, and best friend to the Thin Lead, but that is where the comparison stops in the FGBF trope. Sherman-Palladino's work in creating this well-rounded and loveable character without ever having to resort to cliché or negative stereotyping is nothing short of miraculous in the time and culture within which *Gilmore Girls* was made.

Straight away, when we first meet Sookie, Lorelai establishes that the pair of them have a want and a goal. Together. Not only that but Lorelai also makes it clear that without Sookie she would never be able to achieve their dream, and her concern for Sookie's wellbeing shows that Lorelai considers Sookie her equal in every way.

As we get to know Sookie we find out that she is a perfectionist in all things related to her job. Her kitchen is her domain and she works hard to achieve the highest standard of food and service to her guests. She is professional and efficient (even though she is extremely clumsy) and strives to be the best.

In this set up there are so many opportunities to swipe at the low-hanging fruit, to laugh at the fat woman, and it is never gone for, not even once.

Working around food is a perfect opportunity to show Sookie overeating or gorging, giving the audience a visual indication as to *why* she is fat, but we never see it. Sookie is always fussing and pottering around her kitchen but it is always in the act of preparing food for others. This actively counters the greedy and selfish trope attributed to fat women regarding food.

While Sookie is clumsy and laughs could be easily gotten by her slipping and falling over and lying on her back like an upended turtle, we never see her fall. Occasionally she burns her hand or reaches for the wrong thing, yet the physical comedy of these moments often come from her kitchen staff, darting about in a well-practised dance, moving the sharp things Sookie left unattended or closing open cupboards, all in an effort to protect Sookie from her clumsy ways. This shows that Sookie's clumsy nature doesn't stem from a need to give the audience visual gag punchlines in the form of her physical ineptitude but is a well thought out and tangible aspect to her character.

When it comes to love, Sookie is single and quite shy. In Episode 11 of the first series there is a moment, which I believe to be a breakthrough moment in the treatment of fat women on screen, when Lorelai makes a comment about Sookie not knowing much about relationships because she hasn't dated in years.

There. The set up. The perfect opportunity for Sookie to play the perfect FGBF and to confess to Lorelai that she knows that she isn't as worldly or as desirable as her best friend because of her size.

And it doesn't happen.

I held my breath in the silence that followed the comment, waiting to see how Sookie would react, but I was spared as it was Lorelai who spoke first.

'Wow. Zero to jackass in 3.2 seconds…No, it is not alright, it is never ever okay for me to talk to you like that, I'm so, so sorry.'

I was stunned. A Thin Lead calling herself out and apologising to her FGBF for making her feel, even for a second, that she was in any way lesser.

I had never seen that happen before on screen. I did not expect the show to call itself out for even suggesting that Sookie is a side-line character. Sookie herself admits to not being out there in the dating scene, but it's because her work is so important to her and she knows where her priorities lie. Again, this gives her an impetus and drive that is a valid reason as to why she is not in a relationship that has nothing to do with her body or her confidence.

Later in the episode, Sookie asks out Jackson, the oddball vegetable supplier with whom she has regularly haggles/has screaming arguments. He bashfully but immediately says yes. In the next episode, on their date (which they double with Lorelai and Jackson's rude cousin, Rune) Sookie is anxious and unsure, not because she thinks that Jackson won't fancy her, but because she is worried about her awkward and cooky nature. Her only concern regarding her appearance is that she did her hair up really fancy and was worried that she no longer looked like herself outside of her

47

chef's overalls and signature colourful bandana. She is worried to present anything except her well-honed and loved sense of self.

It takes Sookie and Jackson a long while to get conversations started on their date, but once they get past the awkwardness things go well, despite the awful rude cousin making it a horrible night for everyone, especially Lorelai.

What's also nice about this dynamic is that it is very unusual for the Thin Lead to play the supporting role in a FGBF's romance. I could list ten scenes from other television shows that feature the Thin Lead dragging her FGBF to a double date or a party with the cool kids that she doesn't want to go to (Nancy and Barb, for one), and then proceeds to ignore her friend. It is refreshing that in this scene it is Lorelai who takes the hit for the team and actively has a terrible time, all in support of Sookie's new relationship with Jackson.

Lorelai has nothing to gain or lose with Sookie's relationship, it doesn't have any effect on her and what's going on in her life, so she didn't need to put her episode arc on hold to go along for the ride in support of Sookie – in fact it is really rare for a Thin Lead to sacrifice any sort of time or development in favour of the FGBF, but Lorelai did.

McCarthy's portrayal of Sookie St. James on *Gilmore Girls* was her breakout role into the world of television. While McCarthy is a powerhouse, able to masterfully walk the line between drama and comedy, turning on a hairpin to punch in the emotional gut when you least expect it, the writing of Sookie's character gave her opportunities to show this to the world.

We don't laugh at Sookie; we laugh with her. We laugh because she is relatable, and we relate to her. She is a fully-fledged person with her own wants and needs that exist outside of the central narrative and progress independently of the story line of her Thin Lead best friend. I truly believe that because of this progressive and inclusive writing of Sookie's character McCarthy was able to go onto bigger and better things with the autonomy to demand real characters to play.

After *Gilmore Girls*, Melissa McCarthy went on to star in her own sitcom as Molly in *Mike and Molly*. The show revolves around two plus size people who meet at Overeaters Anonymous and develop a relationship.

I knew very little about this series before sitting down to watch it, and I was unsure about whether I would enjoy it. The fact that it was a Chuck Lorre creation that centred around fat people made me uneasy. Having seen several episodes of *The Big Bang Theory*, I knew that Chuck Lorre's style when it comes to sitcoms was to pick a societal group (nerds, fat people, bad mothers) and to throw out the most obvious jokes and clichés about that group, script after script, and call it a comedy. All any *Big Bang Theory* joke needs is a big scientific word, an element from the periodic table and a quote from *Star Wars* and the studio audience will laugh and assume that it's geek culture, no matter if the joke even makes any sense.

Mike and Molly is very like this but replaced all geek jokes with fat jokes.

My back teeth were clenched as I hit play on the pilot episode, anticipating the worst kind of fatphobia played out for a studio audience laugh.

The show opens with police officer Mike and his partner, Carl, who hands out joke after joke, hit after hit, about Mike, his weight and his size. Mike just sits there and takes it, occasionally hitting back at Carl, slagging him for living with his grandmother, but it's weak and repetitive. The first five minutes of the show and the introduction to Mike is an exercise in cramming as many new and inventive ways to mock a fat person as possible.

After this scene, it's time to meet Molly. My teeth clenched further in fear. I have known and loved McCarthy from her role in *Gilmore Girls* for such a long time and I really didn't want to see her torn down in the same way that her co-star just was.

I was pleasantly surprised.

McCarthy is introduced working out and singing on the cross-trainer. Her mother, a thin mutton-dressed-as-lamb red-headed woman comes out of the kitchen with a huge slice of chocolate cake. Molly watches her mother tuck into the cake with envy. Soon after the pair are joined by Molly's younger sister Victoria, a perpetually stoned thin woman. Victoria tucks into the cake too, much to the dismay of Molly who complains at being tortured by the pair.

Molly's mother and Victoria are supportive and kind. They tell Molly to not punish herself and say she shouldn't feel bad about her size as it has a lot to do with her genetics, reminding her that her father lived in a bigger body.

I felt my jaw slowly loosen and my muscles unclench at the kind treatment of Molly. Contrary to the treatment of Mike, which was just flat out mean, Molly is treated by her family with kindness and understanding, and while there are a few obvious jokes that play to canned studio, the acknowledgement of genetics playing a part in Molly's weight, the acknowledgement of *anything* playing a part in Molly's weight beyond a penchant for overindulgence, greediness and sloppiness, was not what I expected from this show.

While at Overeaters Anonymous, the 'Meet Cute' for *Mike and Molly*, Mike does a 'share', where he talks about his progress throughout the week. He is funny and charming and more than a little self-deprecating, and his humour is what attracts Molly to him. When they chat after the meeting, Mike explains his humour as a way of self-defence, stating that if the others in the group are laughing then they aren't mean because they are hungry. He literally admits to offering himself up as someone to laugh at to gain favour and social currency (which I guess worked, because it caught Molly's attention).

Once again exposing how the two leads could not be treated more differently by the writers, towards the end of the episode Molly does her 'share' and expresses that she loves herself and has absolutely no problems with the way she is, she just has an unhealthy relationship with food that requires some extra support.

Molly establishes herself in the story and in the series as a responsible, capable, generous and loving human being. I cannot stress enough how different the treatment of Molly is compared to the treatment of Mike within the first series of the show.

While Mike and Molly face similar challenges in their blossoming relationship, struggles with their weight, their living situation and their families, throughout all of this, Molly is never directly mocked for her weight, jokes are never poked at her and she is never brought down for any of her choices. She is treated with a level of respect and kindness that, sadly, I did not believe the show was even capable of before watching it.

I wonder why the treatment of Mike is so different to the treatment of Molly.

Is it because the actor is a newbie? Is it because it's easier for men to shrug off these comments because their worth is not tied to their looks? Or is it because Melissa McCarthy in her portrayal as Sookie St. James had established herself as an actor who could give real depth and personality to any role she approached.

In interviews, McCarthy says that when initially approached about the role she was not interested, as a story that surrounds a person's weight is not interesting to her, but when she read the script, she realised the show was at its heart about a loving relationship, which made her reconsider and accept the role. Despite her initial hesitation, and despite the fact that she had already played the role of half a supporting comedic couple before, McCarthy stepped into the role of Leading Lady in a show that, despite all its flaws, placed a fat couple front and centre as romantic leads, which was surprisingly progressive.

Mike and Molly went on to have six seasons of warm comedy centred around these two people's love for each other. McCarthy's performance as Molly is what won her the Outstanding Actress in a Comedy Series 2017 Emmy Award.

If you didn't happen to see that year's Emmy awards, I would highly recommend looking up this category on YouTube. Amy Poehler, actor and comedian and Leading Lady in *Parks and Recreation*, convinced all the nominees in the category to pretend they were part of a beauty pageant. One by one, as their names were called, these exemplary women in comedy stood when their name was called, fanning their faces and feigning tears (think Sandra Bullock in *Miss Congeniality* levels of theatricality) as they ran on stage and stood hand-in-hand. It was a silly joke but one that had impact. My heart swelled with joy.

When Melissa McCarthy's name was called as the winner of the Emmy, she was surrounded by genuine colleagues and friends who all screamed, cheered and hugged her, gave her flowers and a tiara and were nothing but happy for her success. In that moment a plus size woman surrounded by Thin Leads was celebrated as not just an equal but as a standout. It was a glorious moment for female friendship in film and television and it's a moment I have been fortunate enough to recognise in my own work as an aspiring comedy writer and someone who has been bolstered by my female friends and colleagues.

It didn't stop there for Melissa McCarthy. While gracing the film and television screens with both comedy and drama roles over the past twenty years since *Gilmore Girls* she has shown a depth and range that rivals any Thin Lead Hollywood starlet.

In her more recent career, McCarthy has co-written a number of comedy films with her husband Ben Falcone. While Falcone directed, McCarthy played the lead roles in *Thunder Force*, *Life of the Party*, *The Boss* and *Tammy*. McCarthy's power in Hollywood has given her the autonomy to take the narrative of fat women in comedy into her own hands and shape it with her own nuanced voice. While this style of comedy isn't going to be winning any Oscars any time soon, it demonstrates how fat women characters can be more than the butt of the joke, which we knew already as McCarthy is a staple heavy hitter in several dramas too, such as *Can You Ever Forgive Me*, *Nine Perfect Strangers* and *The Starling*.

A side note here about another plus size writer who was able to change the narrative surrounding the portrayal of fat women on screen: Welsh comedian and writer Ruth Jones who is one half of the writing team behind the charming family sitcom, *Gavin and Stacy*. She and fellow actor, writing partner and plus size creative, James Corden, (this was the show that launched his career) starred in the show as the respective best friends to the titular characters. Jones's portrayal of the gruff and enigmatic Nessa, a broad Welsh lass with a laundry list of job experiences and anecdotes about flings with celebrities to her name, is fresh and hilarious.

While the start of the series has Corden's character of Smithy berate her to Gavin for her size, the pair end up having sex in a hotel bathroom and engage in a fraught and strange relationship, resulting in them having a baby together.

Nessa is an autonomous character who is completely unphased by societal expectations of femininity. While you can draw parallels between Nessa and Fat Amy, the key difference is that Nessa's confidence is never played in a way that suggests insanity or a loose grip on reality. She just flat out does not care what others think.

Because Jones was the one to author the character of Nessa she approaches her with lived experience, with wants, ambitions and cares. She is the first to tell anyone off for raising their voice to her, she is very open about her number of sexual partners, many of whom are international people of interest (member of the House of Lords John Prescott for one), she has a number of jobs and is queen of the hustle (telling fortunes and being Santa are just two of her jobs). Nessa is so much more than just a thing to be laughed at for the purpose of comic levity, she is able to fulfil her purpose and still be a nuanced character. We need more characters like Nessa, and therefore more plus size women in the comedy writing spaces.

In many of the roles performed by Melissa McCarthy you will find positive examples of how to treat a plus size female comedy character with kindness and autonomy. McCarthy is the reason that I know the difference between laughing at and laughing with. She is the reason that I can watch any film that stars Rebel Wilson and grit my teeth in cringe for her, hating whatever management allowed her to do nothing but be a thing on screen to be pointed at, laughed at, and portrayed as crazy for showing any confidence in herself or any sense of sexual empowerment.

McCarthy and Wilson have a history of playing the best friend character, which is not in itself a bad thing. Having films and television shows that centre in any way female friendship is something to be encouraged, and female friendship is an absolute goldmine when it comes to comedy.

I cannot begin to describe to you the number of golden nuggets of pure comedic brilliance that has surfaced in any women-only WhatsApp group thread I have been a part of. I've been a bridesmaid many times – and while these moments are not rarities at all in the private digital space, they are a rarity on our screens.

Sadly, while female friendship in comedies is rare compared to stories that feature male friendships and bromances, many of the female-driven stories have been taken out of the hands of female creators and placed in the hands of seasoned male comedy creators.

While these creators may be experts in their craft, this exclusion of women from the creative process leads to stories that lack any authenticity, nuance and charm. The stories become less about women, but more how women are (negatively) perceived by men, the comedy being derived from the worst traits of womanhood as seen through the male lens.

The things that make female friendships so important to us, a lifeline even, are completely and utterly overlooked in favour of the worst characteristics of women characterised by men.

LET'S TALK ABOUT *BRIDESMAIDS*

I'm just going to come out and say it. I hated everything about *Bridesmaids*. I think it's the worst film I have ever seen. I recall at the time of its release in 2011 the film being heralded by the media, critics and my peers as one of the funniest films they had ever seen, claiming it was '*The Hangover*, but with women'. Both McCarthy and Wilson appear in this film, and in both instances they are treated with utter contempt.

The premise of the film is that protagonist Annie, played by Kristen Wiig, a woman who's struggling to get back on top of her life after her small business bakery went under in the past year, is asked to be Maid of Honour to lifelong friend Lillian, played by Maya Rudolph. Her efforts are undermined when she comes up against serious competition in the form of another bridesmaid; super wealthy and manipulative wife of Lillian's fiancé's workmate, Helen, played by Rose Byrne. As Annie tries to do what's right for Lillian, her imploding personal life means she is not as there for her friend as she should be, and her insecurities spurred along by Helen, cause her to repeatedly let Lillian down. She also has a rather pointless B-plot romantic arc with kind but bumbling local police officer Rhodes, played by Chris O'Dowd.

I thought the concept was a good idea; to explore the highs and lows of female friendships, old and new, using the context of a bachelorette party to underline the extremely gendered behaviour and the expectations and pressures placed on all of the women in the bridal party. I have been a bridesmaid three times, and anyone who has been in similar situations can tell you that navigating this space can be a political minefield, which is why I expected so much more from the film everyone was going so crazy over.

While I could go on for pages about all the things I found reductive, lazy and dismissive about female friendship (and women in general) in *Bridesmaids*, I have no desire to fall down that hole, so instead I will limit my focus to examine the two women I have already been speaking about and their roles as fat female characters in the highest grossing female-led comedy of all time.

Starting with Rebel Wilson; her character didn't need to exist.

She is Annie's roommate, and the first time we see her she shares her new tattoo with Annie, one she got for free from a stranger out the back of his van. It's a huge and infected-looking grotesque worm-like creature with a racially insensitive cartoon face that stretches all the way from her belly around to her back. She lifts her shirt and shows it off and there, within five seconds of her appearing on screen, audiences are invited to laugh at her body and think it disgusting. Sure, the gnarly tattoo doesn't do her any favours but it is a very weak mechanism to encourage the audience to both consider this character disgusting because of what she allows to happen to her body (I'm sensing some fatphobic subtext here) and crazy for thinking it was acceptable in the first place. Something to be proud of.

Rebel Wilson, who is passed off as the sister of other roommate Matt Lucas (who is British and claims Wilson is British despite her blatant Australian accent), is only there to make Annie feel like she is in a terrible living situation, and to raise the stakes when they ask her to move out so they can live alone together, not so subtly implying an incestuous relationship. Annie meets her 'rock bottom' when she has to move back in with her loving, generous and attentive mum. She compared her rock bottom of that to an alcoholic's in a stunning display of straight, white, thin lady privilege, and we never see Rebel Wilson on screen again.

Melissa McCarthy had more to do on *Bridesmaids*. Her performance as the blunt and foul-mouthed but loveable Megan, sister of the groom-to-be is widely considered as her breakout role, more so than her time on *Gilmore Girls*. Her placement as the groom's sister is clever as it allows her to be a wildcard. There's almost a universal understanding that Megan's invitation into the bridal party is one that comes from obligation and not from any real connection or desire. In fact, I don't think the bride, Lillian, ever speaks to Megan on screen after introducing her to Annie.

McCarthy's Megan is not like any of the other bridesmaids. She doesn't wear any makeup and wears clothes that are butch and unfeminine (begging the questions whether the character was queer coded, which is a way to suggest a character is queer without actually having to follow through and therefore alienating a homophobic American audience). In her first interaction with Annie she tells her the story of how a dolphin saved her life when she fell off a boat (ding, ding, ding; physical ineptitude) and how she had a telepathic connection with this dolphin who told her he was saving her life, setting her up as 'the crazy one'.

Megan's clumsiness carries on through the film, as at a dress fitting she awkwardly drapes herself over the back of a couch and falls heavily and awkwardly onto it before getting food poisoning and shitting in a sink. I mean, all the others vomit or shit too but Megan is the only one to pull down her knickers, hoist her dress and be heard shitting in another display of physical ineptitude. This incompetence then transforms into a strange physical sense of sexual empowerment in the scene on the plane where she sits next to someone she suspects of being an undercover Air Marshal, played by McCarthy's husband, and flirts outrageously. Megan uses her leg placed up against a wall as a physical barrier for the passenger coming back from the bathroom, showing her flexibility and giving him access to the 'steamy heat' coming from her 'undercarriage'. While I appreciate showing that Megan has a confidence about her body and is not afraid to wield it (even if she does so in a way so aggressively it's borderline problematic), the films earlier displays of her physical ineptitude discount her body as damaged and faulty from the off, so when she displays this confidence we the audience are meant to see her offer as unappealing and even disgusting.

Megan has one saving grace in the film, and that's when she shows up at Annie's mum's house when Annie is at her lowest point and tries to get Annie to physically fight for her life, engaging in a sibling type wrestling match. When Annie admits to being at her worst because she has no home, no job and no friends, Megan calls her out, saying that she is a friend and she is there, showing up for her when she is not willing to show up for herself.

For me, this is the only positive moment of female friendship displayed in the whole film. Yes, there are other moments of genuine friendship, like when Annie and Lillian are talking about men's propensity to be subtle as a flying brick when trying to get their partner to give them a blowjob, but there are no other moments that are about just the women in the conversation. There is no undercurrent of jealousy, envy, one-upmanship or shame, just a pure moment of connection between one person having a horrible time and the other there to help them through it. It is the first time we see a real and believable depth to the character of Megan, and it is the turning point of the film; the drive for Annie to get up off the couch and actually try to make things right.

And we never hear from Megan again.

Instead of going with Megan and instantly making things right with the bridesmaids (I swear, more than half this film has fuck all to do with bridesmaids), Annie completely sets her aside and tries to make things right…with *Rhodes*! That's right. The first person she decided to make good with (by baking him a cake) is her B-plot not-boyfriend.

It is only when Helen turns up at Annie's door because Lillian has gone missing that she actually tries to make things right with her best friend.

And she doesn't even immediately do that. She uses the excuse to find Rhodes and force him to forgive her, once again placing the romance plot above the female friendship plot.

Megan is not seen again until the wedding. She disappears for the rest of the story. We get some sense of her story having its own ending because we see the Air Marshal sitting in the crowd looking up at her adoringly, but how those two connected between their meeting on the flight and them being dates at this wedding, we will never know. We must assume that all that was happening sometime when Annie and Rhodes were off having a boring conversation.

The female friendships displayed in *Bridesmaids* are steeped in insecurity, classism, pettiness, jealously and closeted homophobia. The very fact that this film is the highest grossing female-driven comedy of all time actually boils my piss because I can find nothing in it, except that one moment with Megan, that doesn't actively reduce and diminish the importance and the female friendship and its place in the hyper heteronormative- and gendered-space that is the Western wedding industry.

And yet *this* was the role that gained McCarthy her Oscar nomination. Since then, she has only been nominated once more, for Best Actress in *Can You Ever Forgive Me?*

It's laughable, but it's sure as fuck not funny.

There are so many plus size women working in comedy today; we are a funny bunch. Because we learned early on it was a way to protect ourselves, we have a natural aptitude for comedy that is not being utilised or even respected by our industry. Despite our natural aptitude to take a bad situation and make it good with a laugh, it's still a rare thing to find stories written by us in the media. McCarthy and Jones are the exceptions, not the rule.

Comedy is and will always be subjective. I know there will people out there who believe that *Bridesmaids* is a breakthrough piece in feminist comedy and find it pee-your-pants funny, and that is totally valid. I'm just not one of them. I think that when it takes you as long as it took me to realise that I deserved more than to be the butt of the joke, it's harder to let people laugh at you and not with you.

Like my granny always says, 'If you don't laugh, you'll greet'.

CHAPTER 5
Until The Fat Lady Sings

Does anyone really know where the saying 'It isn't over until the fat lady sings' comes from?

I always thought it was from opera, but I'm not sure where I got that impression. Maybe it's because my only exposure to opera as a kid was the *Looney Tunes* 'Kill the Wabbit' episode with Elmer Fudd and Bugs Bunny. I'm pretty sure at some point in that episode there is this big plus size woman belting out an aria wearing a Viking helmet with the horns and everything. Maybe I'm misremembering that. Either way, I didn't have a huge access to theatre when I was young.

I had more than a lot of people who lived in my area. I was very lucky that my parents, who are huge fans of live music, would take me to open days at the Scottish National Orchestra, where all the musicians would teach kids about the instruments and composing and conducting. They also took me to the ballet once at Christmas to see the *Nutcracker*, and after I got bored – in my defence I was like six, I love the ballet now – they decided to go with the panto the following year. And I went to a Tom Jones concert when I was in Primary 6, which was an experience; surrounded by hundreds of thirsty middle-aged white women asking me, a ten-year-old, if I fancied the man himself. It was a very varied education in stage-based production.

I remember the first time I felt the full impact of musical theatre and how it could lift me right out of my own body and transport me to magical and wonderful places. I was on a school trip in my first year of High School. We went to London and saw *The Lion King* on stage. Having been a lifelong fan of the original animation (and having a freakish ability to commit whole scripts to memory) I wasn't really expecting much new to be honest.

When the first ringing notes of 'The Circle of Life' were belted out, followed by the accompaniment of the full choir, I felt my soul leave my body. The fullness of the music, the human embodiment of the animals, the revolving stage turning and revealing the majestic Pride Rock and the design that grounded the production in the Serengeti, all of it had tears pouring down my cheeks.

From then on I have loved musicals. My sister and I saved our money to go on day trips to London to see matinee shows, and we would come back floating, our buzz continuing for several weeks as we played the soundtrack CDs on repeat, much to the despair of our parents.

It caused my dad particular pain as he has always hated musicals. When pressed for a proper reason, he said he could never really get into a story that was so shallow that at any given moment the cast could break into a song or dance.

I found this absolute nonsense. Yes, to my untrained ears, I thought the songs usually came from nowhere, and as a disciple of cinema I was fascinated by a story that existed outside of the songs, but I didn't care. It was a medium I could sit purely as an audience member and enjoy, something that I didn't have to analyse or pick apart, I just sat and let it sweep me along wherever it was going. It was Bob Fosse who said, 'The time to sing is when your emotional level is just too high to speak, and the time to dance is when your emotions are just too strong to only sing about how you feel'.

Sometimes words just aren't enough. Conversation isn't enough and sitting to talk just isn't enough to capture everything you have inside. There's a romanticism of musical theatre – known as the 'Magic of Musical Theatre' – a beauty and a whimsy that you just don't see in your day-to-day cutting around the West End of Glasgow. The scummy bit, not the trendy bit.

My High School was in a relatively deprived area but it had attached to it The Dance School of Scotland and Musical Theatre Programme. Kids from all over Scotland would transfer to Knightswood to get a full-time education in ballet, contemporary dance and musical theatre alongside their everyday studies. The majority of these kids were thoroughly middle class. They stayed in halls of residence, had after school support from their teachers, and they all had a separate casual uniform of a branded tracksuit and had queue skipping privileges at lunch so they could spend as much time as possible rehearsing in the studio.

I thought I was posh for having more than one toilet in my house until I met these kids. They made the rest of us look and feel like plebs.

At this point in my life I was in love with musicals and musical theatre, but I've sadly inherited my mother's voice that sounds like a bag of smashed arseholes when in song, and I was plus size and so convinced that I was excluded from the act of dancing as a whole. As much as I loved it, I knew musical theatre was not something that I could aspire to.

That said, we never had the huge advantage of seeing many shows. I did better than most but we were at the mercy of what was touring and how ridiculously pricey the tickets were. As much as I would have loved nothing more than to go to every show that blew into town, most of my musical knowledge and experience came from watching musicals that were on screen.

Screen-based musicals are a funny thing, as they are usually an adaptation from a stage production that has been adapted from another property. By the time it gets to screen it has kind of gone through a sort of Whispering Gallery game when it comes to the story. Take, for example, Roald Dahl's classic story from 1988, *Matilda*.

Matilda was adapted for film in 1996 by Danny DeVito (who also played the father character), and starred Mara Wilson as Matilda and Embeth Davidtz as Miss Honey. In 2010, musical comedian Tim Minchin and playwright Dennis Kelly adapted *Matilda* into a stage musical which has had stints in the West End and Broadway and has had UK and US tours. In summer 2023, Netflix is scheduled to release a movie adaptation of the stage musical of *Matilda*, starring Emma Thompson, one of my favourite actors of all time, as the terrifying (in a fat suit – rant for another time) Ms Trunchbull.

One of the first authors I fell into as a child was Roald Dahl, and I reread *Matilda* and *The Twits* many times. On certain Saturday mornings my parents both had to work, and so me and my sister would go to my auntie's and we would watch *Matilda* and make pancakes during the scene where Matilda made pancakes. I bought my sister tickets to see *Matilda the Musical* in London for her birthday and that was a really great trip. I have a different relationship with every adaptation of this story and because of that I see each of them as separate pieces of work. Not going to lie, I really hate the self-righteous 'the book was better' people when discussing screen-based adaptation. Of course the book was better, the book was the original text! *We get it! You read! Big wow!*

While I know that there is a huge back catalogue of glorious movie musicals from the Golden Age of Hollywood – *South Pacific*, *The Sound of Music*, *Seven Brides for Seven Brothers* for example – I will mainly be looking at modern examples of screen-based musicals. This is primarily because there are few plus size women in these musicals, but also because there is only so much criticism I can do of a previous time and generation without falling down a deep academic media criticism spiral. Literally no one wants that right now.

More modern and contemporary screen-based musicals existed alongside the rise of the body positive movement. At the end of the 90s, the whole 'nothing tastes as good as skinny feels' way of thinking started to loosen its grip on the media, and women in general were not told as vehemently to hate their bodies. This must have had an effect on the musicals created at the time. It's so much easier to break into a song and dance if we do not hate ourselves.

THE TURNBLAD WOMEN

If I say, 'Think of a plus size woman in a musical', nine times out of ten you are going to think of Tracy Turnblad and the musical *Hairspray*.

For those who don't know, *Hairspray*, set in Baltimore in the 60s, is about plus size teenager, Tracy and her ambitions to be a featured dancer on her favourite television show, *The Corny Collins Show*. She auditions and is rejected for being plus size, but afterwards she meets a group of the Black dancers who dance on the show once a month. They teach her some dance moves and at a dance event hosted by Corny Collins she shows them off, gaining Corny's attention and being offered a spot on the show. Tracy uses her place on the show and rising popularity to rail against segregation and fights for the show to become integrated.

The 2007 movie adaptation of *Hairspray*, directed by Adam Shankman, (adapted from the Broadway musical, which was adapted from the 1988 John Waters film) has a star-studded cast including Queen Latifah, Michelle Pfeiffer, Allison Janney, Christopher Walken,

Zac Efron, James Marsden, Amanda Bynes and, of course, John Travolta in the drag role of Edna Turnblad, Tracy's mum.

This is where context and the history of the story is key. The original story is by John Waters, a huge player in LGBTQ+ cinema and someone who often uses drag artists or creates gender-fluid characters in his work. The original is part of the historic culture of queer cinema, with Edna being portrayed as a drag role by iconic drag queen, Divine. In its contemporary adaptations, however, the character for Edna has been reimagined, portraying more of a panto dame role for comedic device purposes, not queer commentary.

The panto dame and the drag queen are very similar, in that both are men dressed as women for the stage, but the essential difference is that while one artform was discriminated against and called criminal until just a few decades ago, the other has been widely accepted as a theatrical device dating back to the 1600s.

Queer Kernow, a Cornish based queer history research collective, argues 'that the reason pantomime dames were acceptable was that a (presumed) heterosexual man acting as a woman for comedic effect; their gender was obvious and therefore not challenging, and they are not celebrating femininity but are ridiculing it. Whereas the art of drag is the exact opposite; it's playing with gender in a considered and thoughtful way rather than as the butt of the joke'.

In the 2007 film, Edna is a sad character. She suffers from agoraphobia and has not left the house in over ten years, citing the reason of being ashamed of what she looks like now, as she used to be much thinner and a beauty queen, and fears what the neighbours might whisper about her. While Tracy, her daughter, is sunshine embodied, embracing all that life has to offer and not letting discrimination against her stand in the way of her happiness, Edna is crushed by just the expectation of negative treatment for her size.

While it is joyous to see Tracy's rise to stardom on the show inspire Edna to take positive steps in her own life, the journeys cannot be fully comparable because the character of Edna is portrayed as a dame, and so everything is played up for laughs, including her horribly stereotypical relationship with food. While I love Travolta's delightfully camp turn in the role, every time the character reacts to a situation it is not grounded in reality but in the 'performance' of a plus size woman.

Edna's eating habits are brought up multiple times in song. In the romantic duet between Edna and her husband, 'Timeless to Me', Edna sings, 'Your hairline is receding. I can't stop eating'. In the relationship affirming 'Without Love' in which the characters imagine the sad state of the world without the emotion, Tracy compares it by singing, 'It's like my mother on a diet'. In the spectacular finale, when Edna dances on television and does an incredible outfit reveal by whipping off her long shirt to reveal a mini underneath, she sings, 'You can't stop my happiness cause I like the way I am, like I just can't stop my knife and fork when I see a Christmas ham'.

It was almost empowering. *Almost.*

Because Edna is constantly linking her size to her colossal eating habits and even though we make no such claims about Tracy it is implied that they both suffer from the same tendencies to over-indulge. While this is a joke for Travolta playing a character in a fat suit, the body of Nikki Blonksy who plays Tracy, Edna's daughter, is tainted in reality.

Hairspray leans very heavily into stereotypes and negative charac-teristics of plus size women because it needs to sell the character of Edna as a grounded presence in this world, while being played by a well-known male actor in a fat suit. I would have less problems with it if they cast a plus size male actor to play the role, *but no, they had to break out the fat suit.*

By doing this they in turn comment on the performer who played Tracy, Nikki Blonksy, as they had the two play off each other as mother and daughter, thus bringing Blonsky's real body into the same realms as Travolta's one which was dripping in parody. The young actress had her work cut out for her in her cinema debut: to play the central role, one of the only 'fat roles' in musical theatre and to do so alongside the ethereal and effortless brilliance of Queen Latifah, and also do so while having her body parodied and made fun of by proxy by Travolta's Edna.

Perhaps the film's saving grace (or the reason I have watched it multiple times, and will continue to rewatch) is the casting of Queen Latifah. In this house *We Stan* Queen Latifah.

Latifah plays the show's presenter and producer, Motormouth Maybelle, and fights for the kids who dance on her show to be welcome to dance on Corny's show. She and Corny are both for integration on the show but they are opposed by the station manager and head producer.

She is a beacon of body positivity, and of power, standing up for the kids on her show and providing a warm welcome for Tracy when she is brought over by Seaweed for a visit. Queen Latifah sings a song of welcome, 'Big, Blonde and Beautiful', where she equates the joys of hosting a good meal with the joys of life. I'm not going to lie, any time I hear a plus size person use food metaphors to express their joy it gets an immediate eye roll from me, but I didn't mind it so much in this instance because it's a bop and Latifah delivers. She is also very welcoming when Edna comes to collect Tracy, although being nervous about being out of the house, inspiring Edna to have a little bit of a sexy moment herself later on in the 'Big, Blonde and Beautiful' reprise.

That said, it does not alter the fact that Maybelle is a 'fat role' and is written with an intrinsic tie to food and appetite, which seems reductive when the themes of the show are as serious as segregation.

It's really not easy for plus size women in musical theatre. There are only so many roles that you are expected to play, all of them 'fat roles' featuring characters that are specifically written as plus size and therefore have their figures somehow tied to the story.

Although a lot of this is because classic musicals will always be performed, beloved and revived, the same stories are being shown over and over again, and we must deal with historic negativity in order to relive the beloved classics.

But what about in the case of new musicals? New and contemporary stories that have all the power to be nuanced and fresh. Musicals that challenge the assumption that you can only go so deep and be so real when there's always a song around the corner.

Maybe these musicals exist, but I'm not going to be talking about them now. Now, it's time to talk about *Glee*.

MERCEDES JONES, THE FOREVER SIDE CHARACTER

As much as I hate to admit it, most of my exposure to screen-based musical theatre growing up came from *Glee*.

Glee was created in 2009 by Ryan Murphy, Brad Falchuk and Ian Brennan and at the start it enchanted people with its quirky tongue-in-cheek approach to setting a karaoke musical in a High School. It even felt like it was meant to be a parody of *High School Musical*, really playing into the low-stakes situations that can be life or death when you are a teenager trying to survive High School. It quickly altered its tone and became what it set out to parody, playing the drama serious as a heart attack then breaking into the most recent Top 40 hit that could be squeezed into the show's production schedule.

While over the six seasons of *Glee* the cast swelled and changed many times with the additions of new competitive groups, new classmates, new exchange students and new celebrity cameos, the original cast stayed for the most part the central figures throughout the show.

One of the core cast, high maintenance overachiever, determined to be a Broadway star, Rachel Berry, as played by Lea Michele, is always central to the story. Her journey from High School nobody to Broadway star is a driving plot, an arc that spans years, and her success also plays into the lives of those around her.

Massive spoiler alert! Rachel gets into the school of her dreams, moves to New York and gets cast in the lead role of Fanny Bryce in a revival of *Funny Girl*. She is followed on every step of her journey to stardom.

The thing is, another core cast member, the powerhouse in training, Mercedes Jones, as played by Amber Riley, goes through a similar journey and yet is not given the same attention.

Mercedes is a plus size, Black singer in the same year as Rachel. She is no-nonsense and powerful, and while she still faces the brunt of bullying that is so rampant in the Ohio High School, she fearlessly takes up space and is the biggest advocate for her own worth.

Mercedes aspires to be a singer, and she ends her journey as a solo artist with so much acclaim that she is one of the opening acts on Beyonce's US tour. This jump from backwater nobody to star of the highest order is just as big as Rachel's, but it is not backed up in on-screen development.

What's more, Rachel is throughout the series always assumed to be the Glee Club's biggest and most obvious talent, and Mercedes challenges that assumption at every turn. I cannot count the number of episodes where the two girls are pitted against each other because Rachel is given a solo or a role or an opportunity and Mercedes makes her compete for it, to prove that she is really the most deserving person for it.

Mercedes, while being friends with Rachel, has to prove over and over again that she is just as talented, if not more so. This is something I can see happening once or twice, but it happens across multiple episodes and multiple seasons that it seems Mercedes doesn't ever really grow as a character on her own. She is constantly there to either nip at Rachel Berry's heels or to be brought out at the end of the big musical numbers at the end of episodes, to be the big belter and give the song that extra bit of gravitas (much like the SeaWorld whales being brought out at the end of the show for the audience-pleasing big splash).

While I cannot say that Mercedes gets no development – that would be hard to pull off in six seasons – her arcs usually involve relationships with other cast mates and are not linked to her career and ambitions. This means that while Rachel is gunning for the big opportunities and applying to schools in New York, Mercedes is trying to choose between two boys in her life. That's not to say that Mercedes is not doing those career-focussed things, but we the audience are not seeing it on screen, and so we give Rachel's journey a higher standing.

Whether it is the creators' choice to bench Amber Riley because of her colossal talent and its ability to outshine the rest of the cast in a heartbeat, or whether it is the creators' own unconscious biases towards the story of a plus size Black woman, I don't know, but Mercedes is sidelined as supporting cast when she should have been the Leading Lady.

If this can happen to Mercedes, who spends so much of her time on screen advocating for herself to hold Leading Lady status, imagine what it must be like for characters in musicals who are actually written as the FGBF.

WHY I HATE *CRAZY EX-GIRLFRIEND*

I was excited to watch *Crazy Ex-Girlfriend*. It was recommended to me by so many people, heralded as fresh, funny and feminist. Needless to say, those people have since been struck off my Christmas card list.

Crazy Ex-Girlfriend, created by and starring musical comedian Rachel Bloom, follows top New York lawyer Rebecca Bunch, as she leaves her New York life, partnership and corner office behind after a chance meeting with summer camp boyfriend Josh. When finding that Josh is leaving the city life behind to go home to West Covina, California, Rebecca follows him in hopes of starting a relationship and a life with him in his hometown.

The show is innovative in its approach to the screen-based musical television format, as we follow a traditional sitcom narrative that has these sorts of breaks in the form of vignettes, almost music videos, where an original song will be placed. The addition of songs is an ingenious way to add into Rebecca's delusion of romance and whimsy; she is someone who thinks that just because she met someone she dated for a few weeks as a teenager it is a cosmic sign that they are destined to be together.

Now, it's worth noting here that in Season Three, Rebecca Bunch is diagnosed with borderline personality disorder (BPD), which reveals the mechanics of the songs from the beginning of the series as a manifestation of Rebecca's mania. However, *without* this essential context, but *with* the acknowledgement that Rebecca suffers from poor mental health and decides early in Season One to come off her medication, to me it reads a little as playing mental illness for comedy, which leaves a sour taste in my mouth.

Rebecca feels a lot of love for Josh, and it is the driving force for the series, and while the little romantic part of my soul loves the idea that this love can only be faithfully articulated and expressed in song and dance, for me this doesn't come through in the series.

When you have a mentally ill character stalking and gaslighting her High School boyfriend and the people in his life, no amount of the Magic of Musical Theatre can turn that into a story I am comfortable watching.

However, while I don't particularly enjoy the early YouTube sketch web series look and feel of the songs, I do appreciate that this is a very big deviation from form by the commissioners to create a television series around this content, which I applaud. It is the same kind of commitment to alternative ways of storytelling that led to successes such as *Fleabag*. While we can acknowledge that the iconic fourth wall break was not an original idea, it was used in an inventive way that furthered the story. The same analogy can be used for the use of songs in *Crazy Ex-Girlfriend*.

What I find interesting about *Crazy Ex-Girlfriend* is that it tries at every turn to separate itself from other sitcoms as a progressive piece of work. On multiple occasions in West Covina, Rebecca is exposed to a slightly outdated attitude, which she never lets go and very quickly and effortlessly slaps down with an offhand 'that's actually not okay' kind of comment. While I really appreciate this effort, the self-congratulatory attitude that accompanies it is an offence that lingers. In its, 'oh look at us, we're so progressive' attitude, it leaves itself wide open to revealing its unconscious biases. In the same episode Rebecca will smack down an awkward comment when a white person makes a generalisation about Native Americans but will also attend a yoga class where Josh's Hispanic girlfriend will sing a Bollywood type song with heavy Indian influences while painting herself a slut because she is good at yoga.

The way the show handles its self-congratulating attempts at being progressive and feminist reminds me of the bad I'm Not Like Other Girls trope, where women, usually in order to get a man, try and separate themselves from 'other girls', painting themselves as unique and special, while lumping all other women together and collectively putting them down as lesser. It's an old attitude that doesn't acknowledge a culture of women lifting each other up, and *Crazy Ex-Girlfriend* absolutely reeks of it.

You only need to look at the character of Paula, a woman who works at the West Covina law firm that Rebecca decides to join and who quickly becomes her best friend, to see how Rebecca Bunch (and Rachel Bloom) view and refuse to value female friendship.

When Rebecca arrives in West Covina, Paula is instantly suspicious. She doesn't understand why such a shit-hot lawyer would leave her comfortable life and salary in New York to slum it in a less than impressive firm. Rebecca assures her that she just needed a change in pace, but by the end of the first episode Paula manages to squeeze it out of Rebecca that she moved there to be with Josh.

Instead of reacting like a normal person would, which would be to tell Josh to watch out for Rebecca and her ulterior motives, Paula claims that this 'love story' is the most interesting and romantic thing to ever happen in this town. She instantly gives Rebecca's actions validation, and she then swears that she will dedicate her life to helping Rebecca with this task to win back her man.

Yeah. When *Crazy Ex-Girlfriend* writes a FGBF, it writes the dictionary definition of a FGBF.

Throughout Season One, Rebecca, with the help and encouragement of Paula, goes through various manipulative schemes in order to seduce Josh away from his girlfriend, Valencia. All of Rebecca's quite frankly terrible actions are given credence by Paula, always being the one to remind Rebecca that she deserves her dreams of true love and that nothing should stand in her way.

You would think that if Paula has feelings this strong about Rebecca's romantic life they must stem from something in her own life that she is drawing on, right?

Paula is established to have a boring husband who doesn't listen to anything she says and two feral teenage boys that she doesn't like being around. She sums up her life as something she wants to escape from and she finds Rebecca's schemes as the perfect way to do so.

This would be interesting to me if I was able to draw any more parallels in the scenes between Rachel's exploits and Paula's wants beyond the classic FGBF 'I want my friend to succeed' motive. Paula is craving romantic attention from her husband, but she knows that he cannot provide it for her, so she looks elsewhere for that excitement and stimulation. Of course, all that is speculation, as none of that is in any way articulated on screen. When Paula is at home, she is usually on her own in the kitchen performing some sort of domestic task while on the phone to Rebecca. We are physically reminded that she is a passive person in her own house and she is weighed down by the demands of, you know, mother-hood, and she counts everything in her life to be unworthy of even mentioning to Rebecca.

This is what I find to be the saddest thing about Paula. She is so uninterested in her own life she gives up any sort of need to share it with her friend. She is so passive in the show that the creators don't even feel the need to justify her sadness and dissatisfaction with life, they just need to show why she is so available to Rebecca and invested in making her happy; because she doesn't think she deserves any happiness of her own.

The only time Paula is seen to get some impetus of her own is towards the end of Season 1, when she and Rebecca have a bit of a falling out. Paula doesn't think that her advice is being taken by Rebecca, and that her best friend only really needs her as a sound-ing board and not as someone to actually have any input in her life. She feels Rebecca is just going to do what she wants, no matter what Paula thinks on the subject.

Duh.

Paula pushes Rebecca away for a while, establishing her own boundaries away from Rebecca's toxic drama, but in the last episode of Season One, when Rebecca is at Josh's sister's wedding, she wanders around looking sad and lost. Head of the law firm, Daryl, sees this and so goes to get Paula from her house, saying that Rebecca needs her. When Paula gets to the wedding, and she and Rebecca see each other from across the room, their eyes lock and they run towards each other. When they meet it is a mashup of hugs, tears and apologies, both of them tumbling over themselves to renew their friendship and say what the other means to them.

Cut to Rebecca sitting in a seat, speaking about all the Josh drama, and Paula sitting next to her, listening and nodding.

I nearly threw something at the screen.

71

Straight away, Paula is returned to the diligent, listening and affirming FGBF, even after we have just had a tiny glimpse of Paula affirming her boundaries and stepping away from Rebecca's toxic drama. Without even flinching, she is put right back in her place, the Thin Lead (and the show in general) showing they haven't learned anything from the fight with Paula or made any sort of effort to change the circumstances that led to the fight in the first place. Paula's feelings and her self-worth don't matter, not when Rebecca has boy trouble and she needs to talk out loud to someone about it all.

Now, I watched all of Season One, and I have been assured by many fans of the show that it does get much better. Rebecca faces up to her delusions and deals with the consequences of her actions, including completely ignoring the important things going on in her best friend's life. In a later season, Paula, who already has two teenage children, discovers she is pregnant and decides to have an abortion, and Rebecca is too blinded by her own drama to see what Paula is going through. I appreciate finally giving Paula character development that exists outside of Rebecca's struggles, I appreciate the conscious effort to call out Rebecca on her shitty behaviour and I *really* appreciate the inclusion of an abortion narrative that is not played as traumatic drama and plays it for what it is, a totally normal and acceptable healthcare choice. However, I had to drag my ass through seventeen hour-long episodes of unbearable FGBF bullshit where Paula got treated like absolute trash.

I don't care if it gets better, it started out shit and it still got a commission. Actually, it got four commissions. *Crazy Ex-Girlfriend* is one of the lowest rated shows to get so many series renewed by its parent network in history.

I am happy to admit that some things take a while to get going and really find their voice, but seventeen episodes? Absolutely not.

Crazy Ex-Girlfriend proves that when a screen-based musical television show has to rely on tropes and stereotypes in order to ground the story in reality despite the singing and dancing breakaways, they don't just *use* stereotypes, they further the stereotypes. Paula would fill up your bingo card within two episodes. It really is hard to root for a main character who shows over and over again that she won't have your back when you need it.

72

'MUSICALS ARE LIKE PORN'

We've all heard the joke, 'Musicals are like porn'; the plot in a musical is just to get you from one song to the next, just as in porn the plot is there to get you from one sexual act to the next and to stop them from all happening at the one time. This is an extremely reductive criticism of the form, and one I don't agree with at all, but I will say that while I maintain my love for musical theatre, the older I get the more I understand what my dad (and my husband) feel about musicals.

During the summer, when large-scale theatre was starting to come back with a bang post-pandemic, I went to see the National Theatre of Scotland's original musical *Orphans*, which is an adaptation of the Peter Mullen directed Scottish cult classic film of the same name.

The story is about four adult siblings the night before their mother's funeral. One wants to stay and host a vigil while the others have to deal with personal matters on this highly emotional night. The story is entrenched in the working-class Catholic communities of Glasgow, where I am from. There are so many nuances that strike a specific chord with me and remind me of my family, which is probably why I could not get fully into it.

Seeing my history, my heritage, my culture and my family portrayed by actors (some of whom were very obviously middle class), intercut with songs and dances, just made the whole thing ring hollow for me.

There is a very tense scene in which one of the siblings, the youngest one, who after getting a gun from a less than reputable local gangster (and friend of the family), ends up breaking into a married couple's house with the gangster who attacks the husband and threatens to rape the wife. It is then that the youngest sibling turns on him so he cannot rape the woman, and they face off against each other, one with a knife and one with a gun.

Knife violence in Glasgow is an epidemic I grew up with. My city is reportedly the friendliest city in Europe at the same time as being the stab capital of Europe. Gang violence is complicated and tragic and it is always linked to poverty. To see it played out in song while the background chorus of interpretive dancers flounce about the stage waving floaty red scarves made me cringe. This is a story you cannot show when you have to break into a song and a dance.

You cannot encapsulate the lived experience of being a plus size woman in a musical. You cannot boil down a lifetime of cultural oppression into a song. When your body culturally excludes you from dancing, how can you use it as a means of expressing yourself?

Musicals have the ability to transport us to other worlds – the Serengeti, The Emerald City, the catacombs beneath the Paris Opera House – they can take us places beyond the limits of our imagination and speak to us using music as the universal language. They create worlds where it is totally believable for people to, at any point, break into a song or a dance.

If musicals can do all that, is it so outrageous to ask that they imagine a world in which a plus size woman plays the lead role? *This is my essential question.*

When I sit in the theatre and hear the orchestra make sounds that cause my body to break into goosebumps, when I look into the eyes of someone on stage giving me their all, sharing the space with me and taking me with them on their emotional journey using their bodies and voices, I am in love. I feel alive. I don't ask questions about who is in the leading role. Show me a fat Elphaba singing Defying Gravity and I will be as there for her as I would be for Idina Menzel. Maybe it's because we are all there together in the same room, sharing something immediate and electric, maybe *that* is the Magic of Musical Theatre.

I've yet to find it on the screen. Something gets lost in translation, and I am more critical about everything the live performance makes me forget about.

I cannot ignore the essential question any longer.

CHAPTER 6

Fake Out Fat

There's no subtle way of putting it, the 90s and 00s were fucking awful if you were a fat person.

From comedians folding 'your mamma is so fat' jokes into their sets, thin actors being cast in roles written for fat people without altering the script to reflect this, and thin actors in fat suits, it was rare to find a fat body on screen that was not belittled, shamed or parodied.

Hollywood and the Western media have been the main creators and perpetrators of a hostile, cruel and demoralising environment for women on screen, using derogatory commentary on women's bodies to fill column inches, create buzz and sell media. We know this. We understand this. We know that no journalist has any right to pass off negative comments on women's bodies, and yet when we see headlines like, 'So-and-So has really let herself go', we gravitate towards them because of years of conditioning. We are told that this is what we should care about. This is important.

This, of course, is a lie.

The term 'gaslighting' was not around when I was growing up. If you have not heard the term before, it is a way of explaining a form of manipulation and emotional abuse in a relationship. It is a subtle form of abuse, where the perpetrator deliberately misleads the victim, creating a false narrative that causes the victim to question their own judgement and, sometimes, sanity. If you are a victim of gaslighting, you are unsure of your view of the world, and you start to question whether your hurt feelings and sense of wrongness are valid.

Fat people have been gaslit by the media for years.

There is no way for me to dive into examples of film, unhealthy narratives and creative decisions that blatantly bully fat people without feeling the damage this did to me growing up, and the rage of someone who has spent a long-time healing from that damage.

Before reading on, know that if you ever felt picked on by a film, that's not okay. If you ever felt like you were being laughed at for your body, that's not okay. If you ever saw a thin actress called fat on screen and thought, 'Oh my God, if she's fat then I must be disgustingly massive', you are not alone. Many of us had those exact same thoughts and we are well within our right to loudly proclaim that we were wronged.

GASLIGHTING: *CALLING THIN WOMEN FAT*

There's nothing worse than seeing a cheap magazine with a perfectly normal woman on the cover and a huge 'FAT' graphic layered on top of her photo. It's insulting. Of course, growing up there were no images I saw that I nodded along with and said, 'Yup, that person is fat' when they objectively weren't. I trusted what the magazine said more than my own eyes. That's how gaslighting works and it's there in any publication that comments on women's bodies.

Unless you actively avoid the month of December, chances are that you have seen Richard Curtis' multi-narrative 2003 romantic comedy *Love Actually*. It's a heartwarming examination of the highs and lows of loving relationships – romantic, familial and platonic – set against the emotionally heightened time of Christmas.

One of the many narratives explored is that of the new prime minister of the United Kingdom, played by the bumbling but charming Hugh Grant, and how he falls in love with one of his assistants, Natalie, played by Martine McCutcheon.

Natalie is charming, working class and a touch foul-mouthed. The first time we get to know more about her – when the prime minister asks her about herself – she says she was recently dumped by someone who told her, 'No one is going to fancy a girl with thighs the size of tree trunks'. It's the first nod to her size being fundamental to her character.

His growing affection for Natalie starts to become a distraction to his job, so he orders that she be fired. (What an asshole move! We are meant to root for this guy?!) When asking another aide to do it, she clarifies, 'The chubby one?' He hesitates, asking if 'We call her chubby'. The aide says, 'I think there's a rather sizable arse there, yes sir. Huge thighs'.

And I never questioned this.

McCutcheon is not a plus size woman. She is not entertainment thin but would have no difficulty buying clothes that fit from any High Street store. I was watching her on screen, I could see with my own eyes that she was not fat, not even a little bit, and yet for a long time I considered her a plus size actor, because I was told that she was. I believed the blatant lie that was fed to me over what I knew to be true.

This is not the only incident of this kind. Ginnifer Goodwin's character, Connie in *Mona Lisa Smile*, is bullied relentlessly for her appearance and told by co-star Kirsten Dunst's character that she will never find a husband, yet when you look at the two actresses together, they are roughly the same size. The character of Jan in the movie (and the musical) *Grease* was written as a fat character, but they cast Jamie Donnelly, a thin actress, and didn't change any of the dialogue. Andy (Anne Hathaway) was called fat at the start of *The Devil Wears Prada*, Carmen (America Fererra) is treated like a FGBF in her father's life in *The Sisterhood of Travelling Pants*, and both Regina George (Rachael McAdams) in *Mean Girls* and Samantha Jones (Kim Cattrall) in *Sex and the City: The Movie* are both termed fat despite no changes in their weight or appearance.

Why the fuck does this keep happening?!

And it wasn't only in film and television, it was everywhere. I remember very clearly the media going absolutely wild for weeks when images of Britney Spears were released showing her wearing a crop top and low-rise jeans with the tiniest fold of skin on display at her waistband. She was called horrendous fatphobic names, and while I could see she had barely an ounce of fat on her entire body, I was convinced that she had done something bad to 'let herself' get into that condition.

Perhaps the biggest gaslighter of the time was the 2001 movie *Bridget Jones's Diary*, directed by Sharon Maguire, adapted from Helen Fielding's novel with the same title, and starring the incomparable Hollywood starlet Renee Zellweger.

The character of Bridget Jones is synonymous with the 30-year-old woman who has not got her life together; someone who is avoiding traditional heteronormative lifetime landmarks – such as mortgages, job promotions and children – instead spending more time on enjoyment with friends and less permanent pursuits. I'm of course eyerolling so hard when I say that, *as if* committing to friendships is a less worthy or permanent life staple than romantic love! There's not a straight (or bisexual) single woman in her 30s who has not been referred to as Bridget Jones at least once.

The film is a contemporary adaptation of Jane Austen's *Pride and Prejudice* although it cuts out absolutely everything about the bonds of sisterhood and focuses entirely on Bridget (Lizzie) and the two love interests, Mark Darcy, played by Colin Firth, and Daniel Cleaver, played by Hugh Grant. Darcy and Wickham reincarnated.

When we meet Bridget on New Year's Day, she introduces herself to the audience as someone who drinks too much, smokes too much and talks to random strangers. When she is brushed off by Darcy as a spinster (at 30?! As if), she decides it's time to get her life in order. She decides that this is the year she is going to change herself fundamentally and achieve her full potential, the main signifier of this goal being finding a steady and sensible boyfriend. Urgh.

Bridget also refers to herself as overweight. When she publicly discloses her weight to the audience via writing in her diary, 136 pounds, she says that she obviously needs to lose 20 pounds.

Displaying her weight and her goal loss in blatant numbers is terrible practice. Weight and body size are not always synonymous.

Bridget sees her weight as something that stands in the way of her reaching her potential, which is problematic. *If* her goal for the year was to live a healthier lifestyle then yes, absolutely, commit to a form of weight loss that will improve both body and mental health, however by lumping in her weight with things like smoking and drinking, the creators are labelling her weight as a bad habit. Weight is not a habit.

Did anyone else see the big pants scene in *Bridget Jones Diary* and feel seen? *Me too.*

Bridget, while preparing for a night out in which she hopes to seduce Daniel Cleaver, debates whether she should wear a small lace thong which will be more desirable if she gets lucky, or to go for the 'hold-in-with-panel-support' large underwear that she believes will increase her chances of getting lucky in the first place.

We see Bridget pull the pants on over her perfectly average size thighs, bum and stomach and she twists around as if to show the audience her worst parts.

The pants don't hold anything in. They just sit tight on her body. Once again Zellweger is presented as a fat person who has to alter her body to achieve desirability.

But she is desirable already. Daniel Cleaver's interest in her already started when she came to work in a short skirt and tights. Clearly Bridget has no qualms about showing off her body, so why does she suddenly see a need to alter herself to secure this romance.

But secure it she does, for a brief time (no pun intended).

The avid *Pride and Prejudice* fans could see the betrayal coming as the true character of Daniel Cleaver (George Wickham) is revealed, but it's still a heartbreaking scene when Bridget shows up to her boyfriend's house to find him sleeping with someone else. The woman he is sleeping with is tall, American and entertainment thin, and when she sees Bridget for the first time she says to Cleaver, 'I thought you said she was thin'.

Bridget leaves heartbroken, humiliated and put down because of her weight. What's sadder still is that she believes there is an element of righteousness to Daniel's betrayal, because the woman he cheated on her with was thinner and more beautiful than she is, and in her eyes that makes his deception justified.

Before the release of *Bridget Jones's Diary*, the media went wild at the casting of Renee Zellweger. The focus of their buzz was not on how the decision to have a thin American actor play a plus size 30-something from London, but on the fact that Zellweger was gaining weight for the role.

Zellweger's natural body state is that of a thin person so it was a considerable undertaking for her to put this weight on, and all it did was show that she would still look gorgeous if she put on four stone. By making such a huge deal about the fact that Zellweger was 'making herself fat' to play a fat character, once again we as an audience were being force fed the lie that this was a fat character and a fat actress.

We are told that she is fat both in the narrative of the film and outside in the real world, and so we believe it. And we take that belief, and we apply it to other aspects of our lives, including our self-image and self-confidence.

This is not okay.

LET'S TALK ABOUT FAT MONICA

You all knew it was coming. It's time to talk about the dreaded fat suit.

I don't feel the need to explain *Friends* here, even if you haven't seen it you will know enough from pop culture references to understand what I'm talking about, the show was the global phenomenon that graced our screens for ten years, from 1994 to 2004. I remember being fourteen and having a watch party at my best friend's house for the final episode, and then doing nothing but talking about it the next day in school. It was something that had a real grip on our lives. I had all box sets on VHS and DVD, I could recite entire episodes from start to finish, and since all ten seasons were released on Netflix, I've probably done a full rewatch at least three times.

It's something that's familiar and comforting *if* you can blind yourself to its problematic storylines. From Joey's sexually-predative behaviours to Chandler's blatant homophobia, to the coercive control-ridden abusive relationship of Ross and Rachel, the show has not aged well in many ways. The one thing that haunts me and my memories of *Friends* is the joke that should have been a one-time gag that was spun out and woven into the bones of the show: Fat Monica.

Fat Monica first appeared in Season Two: 'The One With the Prom Tape'. The episode revolves around Ross and Rachel finally getting together as Rachel realises just how long Ross has loved her for (bit creepy if you ask me) and that he was willing to take her to prom when her date flaked on her.

By this point, it has been mentioned a few times throughout the previous series that Monica used to be fat in High School. The tape gives the audience a chance to see what that looked like.

Instead of casting two teenage actors to portray the teenage versions of Monica and Rachel, they use Cox and Aniston, dress them in early 80s garb, give them early 80s hairstyles, and the costuming does not stop there. The creators give Aniston a prosthetic nose to indicate these years being 'before her nose job' and they dress Cox in a fat suit. And while Aniston's nose is barely (if ever) mentioned, it's just another piece of set design used to indicate the passage of time, all conversation revolves around Monica's fatness and every joke for the rest of the episode is based around her size. She is in an ugly and frumpy prom dress compared to Rachel's, she is constantly holding and eating food, and her date is a fat person too. She is fat, and therefore she is the joke.

'Some girl ate Monica', Joey cries the first time she appears on the screen, and after Monica defends herself claiming, 'The camera adds ten pounds', Chandler asks, 'How many cameras are on you?'.

So, it happened. It wasn't *that* funny, hardly up to the comedic standard of regular writing on *Friends*, but the shock factor of seeing the tiny Courtney Cox in a fat suit prompted some disbelief and laughter.

That should have been it. Joke over. Close the door. Instead, the creators trotted out Fat Monica repeatedly throughout all ten seasons of *Friends* as if it was their funniest and most original idea ever.

I have a lot of negative things that I could say about *Friends*, but my biggest grievance is just how chronically lazy the writing of Fat Monica is. Monica is a high maintenance, competitive perfectionist, obsessed with cleaning but always the first to offer hospitality and care to a friend in need, but all that goes as soon as the fat suit is donned.

In the special two-parter, Season Six: 'The One That Could Have Been', we see an alternative reality where Monica never lost the weight and was still fat. In this reality, she is a more pathetic version of herself. She is constantly eating and is often seen to be sloppy with food around her face (very un-Monica), and when Chandler is having a bad day she offers him her last KitKat as a show of support, but then finds she is unable to give up the chocolate. The icing on the dogshit cake is that Alternative Universe Monica is still a virgin.

Whether the creators are trying to say that she is completely unappealing as a fat person or that her confidence as one is low, they are drawing a line between her body and her inexperience and her lack of personal intimacy. Fat Monica even has a boyfriend, who is shown to have no interest in sexual relations with her. This is contrary to the first season of *Friends* when writers really leaned into the fact that Monica was hopeless when it came to romance. She had lots of sexual partners but couldn't find a steady boyfriend.

Monica is such a complex character, suffering with varying levels of compulsive tendencies and perfectionism, all stemming from an unhealthy childhood where she was seen as and treated as less than her older brother Ross, and yet in any episode where she wears the fat suit her entire character is reduced to a reliance on food and a lack of sexual experience.

Even though it is clear she is still the same person, the character that we as audiences know and love so well is turned into a caricature of herself, and all her comedy stems from the laziest and meanest form of mockery.

Look! A fat person! Laugh at her!

In interviews, Cox said that she loved donning the Fat Monica suit because it gave her a sense of freedom and all she wanted to do was dance. Twice, over the end credits of episodes, Fat Monica holds an item of food in her hand while dancing and shaking her larger body while the studio audience laugh and laugh.

To me, watching a fat woman having fun while dancing is a celebration of freedom to move and to love your body, and if I was naive I would see this dance and smile, knowing that Monica is happy and fulfilled as a human being, no matter what her size is. However, I sadly know my industry better than that; her dance is just another cheap laugh. She is purely there to belittle, and it is horrible that the creators would take one of their own beloved characters and put her on display as an object of ridicule. Surely after six seasons, Cox earned more than that.

The one thing that keeps me coming back to *Friends* over and over again is the relationship story arc between Chandler and Monica. The Friends to Lovers trope is one I have a personal soft spot for (having known and been friends with my husband for ten years before we got together romantically) and to see them struggle and grow up together, get married, try for a child and to go through adoption, I find their storyline the most compelling, engaging and real of all of the character arcs in *Friends*.

In the alternative universe two-parter of Season Six, Monica and Chandler got together anyway, suggesting that even if things turned out very differently in their lives, they would have still found each other in the end. While this is meant to be a romantic affirmation that the two are soulmates, I can't quite give it that much credit.

To me, it is not enough to see they would have still fallen in love *in spite of* her fatness. That's not enough of a signifier that you believe in this love. The suggestion that Chandler has to overlook something to get to his place of true happiness is hardly the stuff of fairy tales. Also, in this version of the story, this alternative reality Chandler has pursued his dream of being a comic book writer and therefore the roles are switched between himself and Joey. As a struggling artist he is often strapped for money, whereas the returning soap opera star, Joey, is flush and supports his poorer friend. Because of this repeated failure Chandler is a more pathetic version of himself. Having only slept with one woman before Fat Monica there is a suggestion that Chandler's ability to accept Monica's fatness is because his standards are lower as a consequence of his social standing.

This is not the first time that Chandler's love for Monica has been presented as conditional. In a Season Five flashback episode, 'The One With All the Thanksgivings', it is revealed that when Chandler first meets Monica he calls her fat to Ross, which really hurts her feelings. This motivates Monica to lose weight and become very thin within the space of a year so that when Chandler returns the following year for Thanksgiving, he is suddenly interested in her romantically.

This gives Monica's weight loss a motivation: spite.

Like all she needed, after all this time of being fat, was a man to prove herself to.

First, Chandler should find her sexy no matter what size she is; Courtney Cox is gorgeous and secondly, how perfect can a relationship be when it is founded on the condition that she is only attractive when she is thin? I really did appreciate the alternative universe episode spelling out that no matter how their lives panned out, Monica and Chandler were meant to be together, it makes my wee romantic heart flutter, but if I were Monica I don't know whether I could ever trust someone who makes it so clear that they prefer me to be thin.

Fat Monica and the suit she inhabits is so ingrained in the *Friends* canon it is still haunting the show 25 years later, and it opened the door for more ill-considered fat suits to be used in comedy.

Another 00s nightmare is the 2001 Farrelly brothers' picture, *Shallow Hal*. Protagonist Hal, played by Jack Black, is in pursuit of true love but he has ridiculously high standards when it comes to a woman's appearance. Her personality doesn't matter to him as long as she is Hollywood standard gorgeous and heroin-chic thin.

What a fantastic premise for a movie. I hate it. Well done. Excellent start.

On a chance meeting with a hypnotist in a lift he is hypnotised, after which he can only see the inner beauty of the women he meets.

Gwyneth Paltrow plays the love interest, Rosemary. When Hal first sees Rosemary, he is instantly infatuated, as he sees Gwyneth Paltrow as her tall, thin and blonde self. The 'real' Rosemary weighs 300 pounds and is just Gwyneth Paltrow in a massive fat suit. Not even a good fat suit, it is frumpy and horribly proportioned and it makes her look like a burst couch.

In an interview with the costume team (which is still on YouTube; burn the evidence guys!), the designer stated that while he was allowed to 'have fun' with the costume, he wanted to make sure that he wasn't making fun of anyone!

In the film, Rosemary causes several chairs to buckle under her; while on a romantic canoe ride with Hal her side of the boat is so weighed down that he sits at a distance above the water paddling air like being at the top of a seesaw; Rosemary jumps into a pool from a low diving board and causes a tidal wave so high that a kid gets blown out of the water and stuck up a tree. These are just *some* of the unrealistic and stupid ways that she is presented as a fat person. The whole film is just one gag after another where fat people are mocked and ridiculed, it is a travesty that it was ever greenlit in the first place.

Not making fun of anyone, my arse.

While the film was trying to convey a positive message – that inner beauty is more important that outer beauty – they failed so miserably that they have perpetuated the opposite. By showing Gwyneth Paltrow in her thin body and saying this is the embodiment of goodness and kindness, you are demonising fat people as immoral menaces. Once again, Hollywood is leaning into the idea that body type and personality are intrinsically linked, and that fat people have fewer and less desirable characteristics than thin people. You cannot place a woman's personality on a sliding scale of morality, and neither can you do so with women's bodies. Our bodies are not a reward system or social currency. How long do we have to wait for the media to stop treating them as such?

There are so many examples of the fat suit that I don't have enough paper to do a deep dive into even a fraction of them, and while I would love to believe that these disgusting fat suits are a thing of the past, every year or so some new show or film will trot one out and I will want to throw something hard at my television.

2019 saw the release of Netflix's *Insatiable*, the story of Patty Bladell, a High School teenager who was bullied endlessly for being fat, but after being assaulted and having her jaw broken and then wired shut for three months, putting her on a liquid diet, she lost weight and suddenly 'is beautiful'. She uses this change in her body (and therefore her social standing) to get revenge on anyone who was ever mean to her. She does this by entering the world of beauty pageants in Georgia to take down these girls from the inside.

The first episode of the show was so offensive in its characterisation of fat girls that I spent most of it watching it through my fingers.

In the first sentence, Patty, who is known by everyone as Fatty Patty, uses her inner monologue to tell the audience that her whole life she has been hungry. Right there the creators are explaining away her fatness as lack of will power and need to overeat, completely ignoring any other social, economic or genetic factors that could play into her size.

Not only that but at the start of the show Patty wears a fat suit. The suit is not realistic, and it shows her with a protruding hard round belly that makes her look far closer to pregnant than fat.

Patty realises how much better she is treated by society now that she is thin, and it enrages her. She clings to the belief that she can only take revenge by becoming part of the social hierarchy, matching the people who made her miserable, and this is where the show really falls down for me and makes me believe that there was not a single fat person consulted on the writing staff or in the creative team.

Patty embodies another tired trope in fiction, the Reformed Fatty or Formerly Fat trope.

This is another trope that I wish would die in a hole, because most of the time when writers incorporate this into the scripts and their characters they do so to try to convey to an audience characteristics that are often untrue. If you have a Reformed Fatty played by a thin actor, you are supposedly meant to understand that this character has a history of shame and a complicated relationship with their self-image. It also conveys that they are determined and strong willed because they at one point decided to take their own health into their own hands and to 'do something about' their bigger body.

The Reformed Fatty trope is a double-edged sword because even though it used to convey positive characteristics it also suggests that the character has been on a gruelling journey to get to where they are now, maybe to escape a cruel and oppressive society, maybe because they grew tired of hating themselves. It is some-times often thrown in as a sort of bonus fact to make a character seem more pathetic. In *The Office*, after the departure of Steve Carell both Ed Helm and Will Ferrell in their brief turns in the role of manager had revealed about their characters when they were at their lowest or most pathetic that they used to be fat/obese. It's such a random thing to throw in, but it is done so with the hopes of making the character seem more pathetic and needy.

The trope is designed to link fatness to a one-size-fits-all view of the plus size experience as one that is to be left behind no matter the personal cost. Fatty Patty Bladell is the dictionary definition of a Reformed Fatty.

No longer ostracised from society, Patty ponders her future, and all the things she can do now that she couldn't do before. She sits in class and wonders what she is now going to be as a 'former fatty'. As someone who has been crushed over and over again, been made to feel like a lesser form of life just because of the size of your body, no miracle three-month transformation would come with the confidence and self-assurance to suddenly challenge the social hierarchy of High School and rise to the top of it.

Bullying leaves scars that last a long time. If you spend your years never having hot-girl-confidence, it's not something you suddenly get when your body reaches a certain size, it is a learned behaviour. Not that I'm saying you cannot be confident and fat at the same time, not at all, only that we have already seen how easy it is for a High School cinematic universe to be presented as an impossible place to be so. *Insatiable's* creators need to get a better handle on their main characters and at least try to better understand where she has come from. To believe that she would be capable of the acts and atrocities she commits in Season One after only three months of being away from her torturous daily existence shows a woeful lack of understanding and empathy for the victims of bullying.

And don't get me started on the best friend character. Patty *is* the FGBF who became the main character, so obviously *her* best friend character, Nonnie, is gay and in love with her (Urgh!). Nonnie even says, 'This is like every great High School movie ever...is this the part where you dump me for better friends and start making out with all the hot guys?'

Being self-aware of the negative tropes doesn't make you immune to them. If anything, showing you are aware of the tropes and leaning into them anyway is way worse than doing it in ignorance.

87

The arc of the season focuses on Patty redirecting the hunger she insists was the reason she was fat in the first place into a sociopathic need for revenge on her thin counterparts.

In the very first episode of the show the creators are suggesting it is healthier for this emotionally delicate and damaged young woman to have a pathological need to bring down others and hurt them socially than it is to listen to her body and eat when she wants food. It equates a physical need, hunger, to a pathological and sociopathic behaviour. Netflix is presenting fatness as a choice and a personality trait, one on a par with being a literal sociopath. In 2019. *Wow.*

Her journey is comparable to that of Helen in *Death Becomes Her* (played by the eternally gorgeous Goldie Hawn), as she goes through quite a journey from mousey nobody to gluttonous monster to *femme fatale* in the course of the movie. The essential difference is that *Death Becomes Her* is a masterpiece of satirical black comedy by Robert Zemeckis, making a very pointed comment on beauty expectations placed on women, ageism in Hollywood, and the dangers of the cosmetic surgery industry. The depiction of Helen in a fat suit (where she sits unwashed in a filthy chair eating ice cream with her hands and plotting revenge on Meryl Streep's character) is deliberately caricature like and extreme in fitting with the black comedy tone of the film and, as much as I still hate it, I understand and appreciate it's narrative purpose. For *Insatiable's* Patty, the use of the fat suit has no such purpose. The extent of its use is to depict as plain as day how horrible it is to be fat and how badly you are treated by the world for being so. For me, that's a little too real. I go to television for escapism, not to be reminded of such bleak realities.

Twenty-five years after Fat Monica galumphed her away onto *Friends* and we're still seeing thin women in fat suits on our screens, holding bagels and chocolate bars in death grips like it's the only substantial part of their character. Like there is a need to use cinematic language to provide the audience with tangible reasons these women look the way they do, even though these fat suit versions are fantastical and exaggerated representations. To always remind the audience of their gluttony and lack of control.

The issue with these fat suits isn't that they are terrible depictions of what the actors would look like if they put on weight (Can you imagine a fat Gwyneth Paltrow? She would still be gorgeous!) or that they present weight loss as a simplistic choice and act of exercising willpower. It is that when these actors don the suit, they also don an alternative personality that is slovenly, unkempt and sad.

There is an air of sadness and unfulfillment in Fatty Patty, Fat Monica, Rosemary and Helen. Before they have their magical fat-to-thin transformations, the characters demonstrate varying levels of savagery. The exhibiting of these women as fat versions of the character doesn't just comment on size, but on behaviour. It suggests that fat people are disgusting slobs with no sense of self-care or preservation, and that thinness is the way for these people to become civilised and sophisticated. The fat versions of Rosemary, Helen and Patty wear no makeup and have unflattering hair, yet as soon as the fat suit comes off, they are made up to look fresh and dewy and their hair looks like a mermaid's. All three stories equate fat with a complete neglect of appearance, and it's absolutely infuriating.

There is a part of *Insatiable* that was glossed over that I think should have been more thoroughly explored; the audience is shown that you are treated very differently as a thin person than you are as a fat one. That being fat means you are undeserving of basic human decency and are an object of ridicule. And it's your choice.

All you need to do is put down the doughnut and choose a better life for yourself. It's as easy as just taking off your clothes. Otherwise, you deserve this treatment.

It doesn't. It's not. We don't.

THE CURSED CAP SLEEVE

Even when not using a fat suit, costuming departments are able to clearly make their biases known when it comes to fatness. Techniques such a dressing the 'fat character' in frumpier clothes than the 'thin characters' (even when the two actors are similar sizes), changing costuming in obvious ways to mask 'problematic' regions of the body, and using costuming to hide a character all feed into the message that fatness should not be seen in the world.

Take *Ever After*, the Cinderella adaptation starring Drew Barrymore in the lead role. In this retelling of the classic fairy tale, Cinderella's two stepsisters are not ugly, but one, Marguerite, is mean spirited and haughty and the other, Jaqueline, is dim-witted and just goes along with all of her sister's schemes. In the film, Marguerite is tall and blonde while Jaqueline is smaller with brown hair. Marguerite is dressed in vibrant colours like gold and orange, with plunging necklines and fitted sleeves while Jaqueline wears nothing but high-collared earth tone dresses with mutton sleeves and an excess of layers. While the two actors are not that far apart in size, it is clear who the creators are trying to portray as the fat character.

I have touched upon Amber Riley's stand out performance as both an actor and a singer in the long-running show *Glee* but I wanted to mention her costuming decisions, especially when The New Directions (the eponymous Glee Club) competed at regional and national competitions. For the girls, the costume design that resurfaced time and time again was the vintage style dress with a halter neck top and an A-line skirt. Whether this is because it's the easiest cut to sing and dance in or whether the costume designer is just a vintage nut, I don't know, but this design leaves the entire arms and most of the upper back exposed. At every competition everyone would look the same, except Amber Riley, who would have a variation of the dress that covered the tops of her arms with capped sleeves or she would wear the same dress with a cheap-looking bolero over it. In later series, this tactic was also applied to Unique and Lauren Zizes, two other plus size women. While this might have been for the comfort of the actors, the move to single them out this way does nothing to cover anything up, not least the problematic implications the creators make with this costuming. It's not a subtle way to refuse to accommodate a fat body.

Covering up neither hides the actors' bodies nor the studios' attitudes towards them. In the case of Raven-Symoné in the *That's So Raven* era of her career, the actress, singer and songwriter was monitored and pressured relentlessly about her weight. In interviews, she recounts being watched and denied food since the age of seven; and was told by producers during her developmental years when her body was going through puberty that she was 'getting fat'. When you look back at episodes of *That's So Raven* you can see that the main actress is constantly dressed in high necked, long-sleeved, flared and layered clothing, masking as much of her body as possible.

You would have hoped that in the decades since sixteen-year-old Judy Garland was abused by producers and executives on the set of *The Wizard of Oz*, and had spies sent to her house to make sure she was keeping to her diet of coffee, cigarettes and chicken soup, the treatment and control of young women's bodies by older men would have improved.

For years I have been sold articles, listicles, podcasts, adverts and billboards that offer advice on how I can use clothing to make myself seem smaller. Small things I can do to emphasise my 'good bits' and hide all of my 'bad bits'. There was a time that I honestly believed that a pair of Bridget Jones big knickers could dramatically change my appearance and therefore how I moved through the world.

The power these stories have over our psyches must be acknowledged. The ingraining of this thinking is so deep that I still know I feel better about myself when I wear hold-ins to a special event, even if the item of clothing I'm wearing doesn't reveal that area of my body.

Whenever I get this way, I look at myself in the mirror and say this to myself, 'It's clothes. Not an invisibility cloak'.

PREGNANCY, AGEISM AND ABLEISM

I mentioned earlier that fatphobia in film and television is a heavily intersectional issue, but I want to take a second to talk specifically about the intersections of fatphobia and pregnancy, ageism and ableism. The blatant fatphobia that inhabits film and television is not limited just to the experience of people living in plus size bodies, this fear of being fat and the punishment of people who are fat bleeds into other elements of our wider society.

There's nothing I hate more than seeing a pregnancy narrative played out on screen and people using the word 'fat' to describe the pregnant person. The number of narratives I have seen about people desperate for healthy and successful pregnancies while mourning the loss of their thinness and being paralysed by the fear of becoming fat is mad to me. You are growing a literal human in your body, surely if you are okay with this fact and the inevitable change and development of your physicality, you can let go of inherent fears of gaining weight and being seen differently by society, right?

Elizabeth Banks' story arc in *What To Expect When You're Expecting*, the 2012 multi-narrative story that follows a number of (heterosexual) couples on their varying routes to parenthood, shadows Wendy, a woman who runs a baby boutique and speaks often about the miracle of childbirth. After a lengthy period of trying with her husband, she finally finds out she is pregnant, but the joyful period of pregnancy she anticipated does not go as she expected because she is hit extremely hard with uncomfortable symptoms throughout. She feels completely and utterly sick, exhausted and gross at every stage because her pregnancy has turned her body into a hostile environment, and she mourns the fact she never gets to feel the 'pregnancy glow'.

She rails about many things, but mostly about getting fat. This always stands out to me as she is also unable to control her bladder functions, experiencing hot flushes, is completely at the mercy of her hormones and uncomfortable at every step. Compared to all these symptoms, surely her gaining weight does not compare? She always knew she was going to gain weight, it comes as part and parcel of the whole pregnancy thing, so why is she comparing gaining weight with being as bad as horribly embarrassing herself in public with the lack of control over her bodily functions and emissions?

While *What to Expect When You're Expecting* is a 00s rom com, so a lot of its flaws can be totted up to crimes of the times, but sadly this is something that is present even in the most recent of properties.

I am such a huge fan of Sharon Horgan, but her latest television endeavour, *Bad Sisters*, which is about sisterhood and a coercive controlling relationship (yes, Sharon!), things that you would expect from such an incredible feminist writer such as Horgan, sadly falls prey to it. One character, played by a straight sized actress, is pregnant in the show, and her husband teases her about her weight constantly. It was the one thing that put a sour taste in my mouth, especially when it was meant to be endearing and loving and a joke. Like, *why?!*

Pregnant people, can we drop the 'fear of getting fat' narrative when it comes to pregnancy? It's tired, it's irrelevant, and it's really fucking reductive. It's disrespectful to the millions of people world-wide desperate for a child that for whatever reason cannot have one. Your temporary weight gain as you grow a human inside you is a First World problem. Get over it.

On the flip side, I am now going to talk about women post meno-pause.

Plus size women of an older age are thriving in film and television, especially in motherly and grandmotherly roles. This body type when paired with this age has connotations to warmth and care, so it is no wonder that this is one of the only places we can see plus size women on screen in an unproblematic way. Molly Weasley from the *Harry Potter* franchise, Olenna Tyrell in *Game of Thrones* and Nurse in *Romeo and Juliet* are all strong, powerful and caring women and incredible roles that would be any actor's dream. To see them played by plus size legendary actors who happen to be older makes me wonder why similar roles where those characters are younger are played only by thin actors.

You just have to look at the casting of Stephen King's most haunt-ing female character, Annie Wilkes, from one of the most notorious toxic-fandom stories in history, *Misery*. Annie was originally played by Kathy Bates in the 1990 adapted screenplay written by William Goldman and directed by Rob Reiner, and was delivered so haunt-ingly it kept me up for weeks and emotionally scarred my sister for life (to be fair, I was sixteen and had to watch it for school and was too scared so I made her watch it with me; she was eleven) In the 2018 *Castle Rock*, a television multiverse story that interweaves the many narratives and characters from a variety of King's most be-loved properties, a young Annie Wilkes is played by Lizzie Caplin. *Go on. Google them. It will piss you off.*

Could it be that in many cases, these older women characters have had and raised children of their own, and so the creators are saying that a woman's appearance might not be as much of a concern to her once she has the more pressing and important societal role of caring for her children? Or maybe once women are past a certain age, they have lost their potential to be sexy, and therefore do not need to remain thin if they don't want to? In case you can't tell, my tongue is positively wedged in my cheek as I write this.

And then there is the intersection of fatphobia and ableism.

I'm not saying that fatness *is* a disability because, while some people living in fat bodies might also be disabled and fatness can add to a person's experience of disability, many are also not. However, both fat people and disabled people live in marginalised bodies, and therefore are treated negatively by wider society.

The taking up of physical space, either by plus size people or by people with disabilities that require mobility aids or other spatial accommodations, is not an inherently negative thing, but it is communicated to be one in the lack of accessibility to spaces that both groups face.

The comparables between the treatment of plus size bodies and disabled bodies are many and similar. The idea of living an able-bodied life being seen as 'the norm' isolates disabled people and ostracises them as not normal. In the same way, thinness is seen as the norm and fat people are ostracised for being not normal.

Fat people are much more likely to receive medical gaslighting and be misdiagnosed in healthcare, they are much more likely to be passed up for a promotion or fired for their weight. They are much more likely to be bullied and to be presumed lazy and lacking in willpower.

The global organisation, World Obesity released a report in 2018 highlighting the media's role in perpetuating weight stigma globally, stating, 'Obesity is highly complex and results from a multitude of factors, and yet a lack of understanding of these complexities means that people with obesity are often blamed for their condition. People with obesity are experiencing abuse and discrimination because of their weight. Weight stigma has become a serious concern and it's being perpetuated across populations, affecting people's life chances and their health.'

And all this is even more true for people who sit on the intersection of both fat and disabled.

Too often is the word 'healthy' thrown around when really what society means is 'normal'. I am fat and extremely fit and healthy. I would lay out here my diet and exercise to prove this claim, but quite frankly it is nobody's business. You do not get to look at my body and make assumptions about my lifestyle, and even if you did and all your assumptions were correct, I am still a human being, deserving of kindness, respect and access.

We all deserve kindness, respect and access.

I am an able-bodied woman and would never presume to speak on the lived experience of disabled people, but I can see and acknowledge that the continuously perpetuated ideals of perfection pushed on us by the Western media excludes us both.

While I am delighted to see a much bigger push for disability representation in UK television programming, Channel 4 championing this with their latest round of *Comedy Blaps*, the same kinds of pushes are not being made for plus size representation in the media.

Even though there are so many similarities in the way the mainstream media treats fat people and disabled people, generally the difference is there are no assumptions that people with disabilities are at fault for those disabilities.

HOW LONG CAN WE KEEP IGNORING THE ELEPHANT IN THE ROOM?

How can any true movement for body positivity and inclusivity on screen happen when we, collectively as an audience, are still going along with the obvious lie that these thin actors are fat? The repercussions of this include generations of plus size women having a warped perspective of their own bodies.

What's more concerning is that in some contexts the literal meaning of the word 'fat' is overlooked and the purely connotational definition of the word is applied to certain people and scenarios to depict a character's personality or even morality.

Ari Sandel's 2015 film *The DUFF* proves this. An adaptation of a book of the same title, *The DUFF* centres around Bianca Piper, a senior in High School who realises that she lives in the shadows of her two best friends, Jess and Casey, who are both considered to be a lot hotter than she is.

DUFF stands for Designated Ugly Fat Friend. A friend who is a DUFF has the responsibility to function as a buffer between her hot friends and anyone who is trying to score with them. The DUFF is usually friendly, approachable and funny, so anyone who wants information on the hot friends can get it from a reliable source. The understanding is that the DUFF benefits from this arrangement too, as the people who are wanting information on the hot friends are (presumably) on the same level of hotness as the hot friends, and therefore out of the DUFF's league. By being the gateway to the hot friends, the DUFF is rewarded for their services by getting attention from and talking to people way out of their league.

The film places its entire construct on appearance and has nothing to do with personality. What's more, it acknowledges that the person in question doesn't have to even conform to the description laid out in the label, they just have to be comparatively less attractive than the hot friends.

In the film, Bianca Piper is played by the powerhouse of YA film and television, Mae Whitman (*Scott Pilgrim Vs the World, Avatar the Last Airbender, The Perks of Being a Wallflower*) who, I cannot emphasise this enough, is *not* plus size.

When she learns from the most popular guy in school, Wesley (who she is not intimidated by because he is also a childhood friend), that she is seen by her peers as a DUFF, she is horrified. To illustrate the point Wesley points out to Bianca another of their peers who is considered to be a DUFF; a petite blonde girl who is friends with a tall leggy girl who could be a supermodel. When Bianca tries to say that this girl is not a DUFF, she is 'cute', Wesley counters that her friends are 'hot', which makes her a DUFF by comparison.

Later, when Wesley tries to apologise for upsetting Bianca, he justifies his actions by saying 'I would never call anyone ugly or fat, that is so messed up'. So, even though Bianca is neither ugly nor fat, since she is less conventionally pretty than Jess and Casey, she is assigned a lesser social status for being such. What's more, to make the concept of the DUFF universally understood, the attributes picked to quantify the phenomenon are 'fat' and 'ugly'.

Fat is not a personality trait; it is a physical thing that you either are or are not.

Bianca believes that the only way she can be seen as 'dateable' and not 'approachable' is to remove herself from her two best friends who apparently make her look bad simply by comparison. After cutting herself off from her support network she gets ostracised even more. She is a victim of cyberbullying and when she finally makes any headway with her crush she quickly realises that he, like everyone else, is using her crush as a way to get closer to and date her friends. She becomes completely alone. In the end she goes back to her friends to apologise for her behaviour, explaining what caused her to try and crawl out from under their shadow in the first place.

Not only does she not get her glow-up, but she acknowledges that it is not possible to glow up in High School; you are the way you are and you should just accept that. DUFFs of the world, aspire to nothing. If this is the ending that Mae Whitman, a girl who is not thin but by no means fat, can hope for, what about the ones who actually are fat?

I'm so damn angry.

I get to be mad. I get to rant and rail. I get to call out all these things for being horrible because they have always been horrible, and I had to live with the consequences. At the time, no one was inter-ested in the damage that was being done, but the world is starting to wake up to the body positive movement and acknowledge the toxic traits of the past. It's not enough. You cannot sweep decades of emotional abuse, bullying and trauma under the rug and call it progress. Amends must be made.

If the character of Bianca was actually portrayed by a plus size actor, would this story be a triumph of representation, having a plus size woman in a leading role? Or would it be just one big reminder that women who look like me do not deserve their time in the limelight?

There was a time in my twenties when I lost weight because my mental health was very low. I was very ill and I didn't share my illness with anyone, ashamed of my own sickness. It was then, when my body felt least like my own and I felt like a tourist in my own skin, that I was treated the best by people around me.

Everyone assumed that I was finally making good choices and congratulated me on my fortitude and willpower. Not one person asked if I was okay, because they all thought this version of me was still the healthiest version I could aspire to.

Distant family members I had not spoken to in years, passing acquaintances, people I didn't even really know, hailed me with comments such as 'You look great', 'Keep going', 'Whatever you're doing is really working for you'.

I realised then that these people would much rather see me thin and sick than fat and healthy.

I don't hold it against them, not at all. I don't for a second doubt that these people in my life really only wanted the best for me and for me to be happy and healthy. What makes me sad about the way I was treated is that the unconscious biases towards plus size people are so deeply ingrained in our collective consciousness that the people in my life, people who have known me all my life and know that I am a confident and body positive person, still saw me as sick and it made them happy for me.

That is the power that gaslighting has, it takes what we see with our own eyes, what we know to be true and it warps our views of reality. It makes us doubt what is real.

I knew I was sick at the time. I knew that there was no way for me to regain my former health and quality of life without putting some of the weight I had lost back on, but I still thought that I was wrong. I thought that I would feel better eventually, even if I had to get sicker to get there. I believed it with everything in me.

Gaslighting begets gaslighting and these lies are getting old. At least 9% of the population worldwide have been affected by eating disorders. Fewer than 6% of people with eating disorders are medically underweight.

Don't tell me these lies don't have consequences.

CHAPTER 7

Animation

In 2017, for her work on *The Beguiled,* Sophia Coppola became the second woman in history to be awarded Best Director at The Cannes Film Festival. What should have been the top story of the festival, this landmark victory for women in cinema was tragically overshadowed by a marketing blunder for an upcoming animation.

Billboard marketing at Cannes is prime real estate, so when a studio purchases the space they mean to capture attention and drum up buzz. I don't think, however, that the South Korean animation studio Locus Creative had any idea their advert for upcoming 'parody with a twist' *Snow White and the Red Shoes* would cause such a stir.

In their ad, there are two versions of the character of Snow White looking at each other. One version, the one wearing the red shoes, is tall and slim with big, upturned eyes, an angular face and impossibly thin limbs and waist – classic 'princess proportions'. The other version, the one holding the shoes, is shorter with a beautiful chubby face, and is plus size.

The copy on the billboard read, 'What if Snow White was no longer beautiful, and the Seven Dwarves were not so short?'

In one line of marketing copy this film, whose target audience is children, equates plus size with ugly. And then blows up this opinion for the world to see at the most prestigious film festival in the world.

The scandal provoked outrage online across the globe. 'How did this get approved by an entire marketing team?' asked plus size model and activist Tess Holliday. Several people stated an intention to boycott the movie because of this faux pas, genuinely baffled that this kind of ignorant fat shaming could still be going on in 2017.

It was around this time that I was working on a pitch document for a children's animated series. There was some call out or another that was inviting new writers to submit ideas for the next big children's adventure series. As someone who was raised on *The Mummy Animated Series, Avatar: The Last Airbender* and *The Jackie*

Chan Adventures, writing a children's animated series has always been an ambition of mine, so I was in hardcore research mode watching as many pilot episodes as possible.

In my research, I came across *She-Ra and the Princesses of Power*, a collaboration between Netflix and DreamWorks and written by ND Stevenson. I was intrigued as I had vague memories of He-Man, She-Ra and Skeletor from when I was very young, but only for their not-very-progressive character design: a well-oiled muscle man and a leggy blonde in a leotard so high in the hips you could see her breakfast every time she did a backflip (if you don't know what I'm talking about here don't watch the show, just Google the Money-SuperMarket ads, they are way more fun and just as camp).

It was because of this I was so intrigued, and so surprised to see Stevenson's name attached to it.

--Both *Lumberjanes* and *Nimona* are graphic novels featuring excellent representation for body types and for queer characters (or course I was hooked on both) so, out of curiosity, I watched the first episode of *She-Ra and the Princesses of Power.*

It was breathtaking. Such beautiful animation, gorgeous colours, hilarious dialogue and, most refreshingly, the characters looked like people.

In the pilot episode you were introduced to a number of women, and all had varying sizes and body shapes; from the thin and limber cat-person Catra to the thick-thighed rebel fairy Princess Glimmer and background plus size Princess Spinderella. And of course, Adora, an average-sized heroine who transforms into the ten-foot warrior She-Ra through the power of a magical sword.

It wasn't until that moment, sitting and tearing up at the end credits music of this pilot episode, that I realised I had never seen a main character in an animation who looked anything like me.

My conditioning didn't start with the FGBF trope in YA fiction, it started much, much earlier.

As a child of the 90s I was front and centre for an incredible decade of Disney animation. *The Little Mermaid, The Lion King, Aladdin, Mulan, Beauty and the Beast, Hercules* and *Tarzan* were all released before I turned ten years old, and those were some powerhouse stories that had a huge hand in my development.

And behind all amazing animation are the animators. Glen Keane, the legendary Disney animator responsible for creating characters such as Ariel, the Beast and Tarzan, refers to animators as 'actors with a pencil'. These introverts slowly bring characters to life with every meticulous scratch on the page.

Of course, the animators aren't the only ones involved. There are character designers, layout and background artists, writers, musicians and so many others involved from the start to finish of the process. All of these people make choices that have a direct impact on the story, and how a blank sheet of paper transforms into a rich and full world.

Animation is a medium in which the only limit is the imagination. Anything that these artists can fathom in their minds and recreate on the page, they can make real. It is a real gift. And a very lucrative industry.

When *Frozen* was released in 2019 it earned $1.28 billion at the box office, becoming the highest grossing animated film of all time and the fifth highest-grossing film of all time. With such a huge audience of impressionable young people at their fingertips, you would hope that the animation industry takes its platform seriously, and uses it to champion diversity and inclusion, right?

LIMITLESS IMAGINATION

The Disney Princess trope is an establishment that has been upheld since the late 30s. To date there are 60 films that are in the Disney Animated Classics series, and of them fifteen feature a (human) Disney Princess figure; the first, the 1937 *Snow White and the Seven Dwarfs* and the latest (at the time of writing), the 2021 *Raya and the Last Dragon*.

In the 84 years between these two films, the design model of the Disney Princess has changed very little. There is no variation on the body type or the proportion size of the characters from film to film; the same oversized eyes, angular face, tiny waist and elongated limbs feature repeatedly. The same standard of beauty from the

30s/40s is still upheld. This perpetuates an unrealistic ideal of perfection. And while there is a lot I could say about how this is received by young boys and how it shapes their expectations of women and girls, I'm going to be focusing on how this ideal is still force fed to young women and girls all over the world at a time when their perception of self-image is very impressionable.

There is room to interpret these character design decisions as justified. *The Illusion of Life: Disney Animation* is a book written by Frank Thomas and Ollie Johnston, two animators who were the lead character designers on some of Disney's most famous properties from the 30s to the 80s. The book is still known in the industry as 'the animation bible', for its detail on how Disney perfected their process and how 'the Disney look' became instantly recognisable globally. Part of that iconic look is the design of the Disney Princess.

The book details the 'Twelve Principles of Animation', which are the rules every action, character or moving object has to follow to make the animation believable and appealing to the human eye. Principles such as 'exaggeration' and 'squash and stretch' are rules that over and under emphasise proportions to aid in the animator's task of creating believable life and movement within the sequence of drawings. With this in mind, it can be accepted that human proportions will be slightly over or under exaggerated in service of the story.

This in itself is not damaging, but when the influence of these exaggerations extends into real life, this is where the stories that children are exposed to start to become harmful.

Comic book adaptations and the Marvel Cinematic Universe spend so much money, time and energy on pushing its actors to their physical limits in the name of faithfulness to a piece of 2D art. The more this happens, the more this unrealistic and damaging image is presented as normal, attainable and desirable.

This tradition can change at *any* time. The animators can draw whatever floats through their imaginations.

What does it say about the industry and our society that it is easier to imagine real life people adopting an expensive, time-consuming and traumatic culture to change their physiologies, rather than ask an 'actor with a pencil' to simply draw a princess differently? What does this say to our children?

Plus size women are so rare in the world of animation, it is easy to just presume that the representation is not at all present. There are, however, many references to the plus size experience within animation that makes a very staunch comment on the social condition of such a physique, even though it hides a lot in plain sight.

I have noticed this commentary come through in the use of magical transformation, through using plus size characters in non-human bodies, and the many varieties and characteristics of the classic villain. It took lining up all these examples and looking at them in the context of one complete collection for me to see the commentary, and for me to really understand how early the conditioning and fatphobia is fed to our children.

I missed it as a kid. I gobbled up these stories both as a child and in my adulthood, and never realised that it had an effect on me and how I saw myself growing up. Stories about witches, dragons and curses and spells, adventure and true love, stories that kept me dreaming and imagining and inspired me to tell stories of my own. I imagined myself as a writer and a spinner of tales, a bard and a minstrel.

I just never once imagined myself as the princess.

TRANSFORMATION AND THE MONSTROUS

Let's face it, everyone loves an iconic villain.

The villain is the driving force of any narrative, their dastardly plots and evil schemes causing our heroes to undergo a series of challenges and trials, putting their courage to the test to emerge victorious over the villain.

In some animations, the villain character is so important, and their want is so integral to the main story that they are introduced even before the main character is, as is in the case of *Aladdin* and *Tangled*.

Because the villain must be an active character in the development of the narrative and they need to have several interactions with the hero, they must have some kind of 'normal' appearance, otherwise the hero would not interact with them in the first place.

In the case of the divine Ursula from Disney's *The Little Mermaid*, she is charismatic and inviting, getting Ariel to trust her despite her awful reputation. Madam Mim in *The Sword and the Stone* first appears as the kindly old woman who looks after Arthur in bird form when he accidentally flies down her chimney. Maleficent, the witch with the scary headpiece and the creepy crow for a sidekick from *Sleeping Beauty,* rocks up to Aurora's christening and curses her in her cradle because the King and Queen didn't invite her to the party (that's some serious Diva Energy).

All these women, while powerful and fierce and a little bit scary, show up in the plots of their respective films ready to cause trouble, and yet the audience must maintain the belief that they can still be defeated. As the plot develops the tension and the stakes get higher and the villains get increasingly scary. At the climax of the film, the protagonist needs to face overwhelming odds and that's when these villains need to be shown at their maximum power, making all hope seem lost for the heroes.

Because we have gone through the narrative with these villain characters we have gotten used to them, so something has to change in order for us to have our perspective of them change, for them to become scarier and more threatening. They have to step up their game.

They need to transform from a mere villain into a life-threatening monster.

In the case of both Maleficent and Madam Mim, they use their powers and transform into huge fire-breathing dragons. In the case of Ursula, she simply becomes herself, but huge. She grows to monstrous proportions, rising out of the water, tentacles everywhere like a kraken. The biggest threat she possesses isn't her magic but her size.

While Maleficent, tall, thin and elegant, doesn't have qualities that the audience would consider threatening in her human form (although her choice of hats and her kind of green-tinged corpse coloured skin always freaked me out as a kid), when she transforms it is into a mythical monster far away from her original character design. For Ursula no such deviation was needed.

I called her divine earlier, and that was deliberate as her character design was based on the queer icon, Divine. Once again Disney employs queer coding to imply villainy and the monstrous; it's horribly concerning, and they aren't making any effort to hide the blatant homophobia. Although it could be argued that Ursula was already part monster by having the lower half of an octopus in her character design, that doesn't set her apart from the rest of the kingdom of mermaids and mermen in Atlantica that Ariel originally hails from. You could argue that Ursula falls under the umbrella of 'mermaid' as a being with the top half of a human and the bottom half of an aquatic creature, whether fish, shark, octopus or other. So, if we take her Mer status as 'normal' as we have done with Ariel, then the creators simply use her original body as the main source of threat when blowing it up to a hundred times its original size.

Transformation stories are a form of body horror, and they play into those fears and, perhaps unwittingly, these stories of transformation when presented to young girls have more impact on their development than we would like to imagine. When fed to young girls, pre-puberty, you are teaching them to be afraid of their own development.

In the grown-up world of horror, the genre has been used throughout history to reflect the fear of their society at the time of their creation. Whether it's stories like Gaston Leroux's 1910 novel *Phantom of the Opera*, warning women with loose morals who are tempted by voices in the night that following those voices will lead to being kidnapped by a monster, right up to the string of 1980s slasher movies telling teenagers to be afraid of sex and the 'psycho next door', horror and body horror is used to tap into our deepest fears, and much of that is rooted in both physical and mental ableism. When every killer is either described as having an undefined mental illness (Michael Myers in the *Halloween* franchise) or live on the outside because of a physical disfigurement (Ruben in *Midsommar* and Professor Henry Jarrod in *House of Wax*) it's clear the fears in the psyche of our societies stem from not being 'normal'. Are we surprised this is the case when we set the examples and standards of perfection on young children, and underline the importance of aspiring to it?

While it would be easy to point the finger at the Disney Princess and blame it for its upholding of unrealistic beauty standards in animation, even narratives that actively deviate away from this storytelling mould can be guilty of unkind behaviours. Moreover, narratives that are actively trying to deconstruct the harmful tropes often fall prey to them.

I was eleven when *Shrek* was released. I can't remember if I saw it in the cinema with friends first, but if I did the memory has been completely erased by the memory of watching it with my parents and sister in our living room later.

When the show *Grumpy Old Men* first came to television in 2002, the following years were a curse for my dad. Every birthday, Christmas, Father's Day or any kind of celebration warranting acknowledgement with a card, was a branded reminder for my father that he is a classic 'Grumpy Old Man'.

My dad has a sense of humour that was wasted on me as a kid. Growing up he was the disciplinary parent, so I have a lot of memories of his grumpiness, but I think I only really got to fully appreciate his overwhelming capacity for joy and humour as an adult.

I caught glimpses of it growing up. The first time I realised my dad had such a deep well of laughter in him was when we watched *Shrek* together, as he physically fell off the couch laughing.

Shrek was a global smash, premiering at the Cannes Film Festival and selected to compete for the Palme D'Or, the first animated film since Disney's *Peter Pan* to do so. The film won Best Animated Feature that year and instantly established DreamWorks as real competition for Disney and Pixar.

Shrek is a parody of several fairy tales, all existing in the same universe and focusing on the main titular character, who is an ogre and on the outskirts of these fairy-tale creatures' society. The film in its approach specifically parodies other adaptations of fairy tales, primarily the ones adapted and animated by Disney.

Shrek loves and relishes his solitude. He is deemed by the world to be 'a great big, stupid, ugly ogre', and rather than waste his time trying to prove himself as anything otherwise, he secludes himself in his swamp – quite content to leave alone and be left alone by the world outside knowing it is the only way to shield himself from their contempt.

The film does not try for a second to hide that it is a parody of the Disney animation empire, placing characters that have been the jewels in the crown of the Disney movies in the background such as Snow White and Pinocchio. It not only alludes to Disney's characters, but to their tropes too. That being said, while the parody elements of the film rehash many images and themes we have seen many times before, the creators decided to take a fantastically fresh approach with their Leading Lady (and Shrek's love interest), running as far away from The Disney Princess tropes as they could. Princess Fiona is fierce, fun and delightfully fresh.

Locked in a tower in a faraway land (hiya *Rapunzel*) guarded by a fire-breathing dragon (I see ya *Maleficent*), Fiona awaits rescue from her true love; the one to slay the dragon, free her and share with her true love's kiss.

When Shrek first crashes through her tower, talking donkey side-kick (Donkey) by his side, Fiona tries to make an appealing first impression by grabbing a bouquet of flowers, straightening her hair and dress...and pretending to be asleep. When Shrek approaches, Fiona even puckers her lips, inviting him to kiss her. Of course, Shrek, having basic human decency, does not kiss the sleeping woman without her consent, but shakes her roughly awake and tells her to come with him.

After the daring if somewhat unconventional rescue from the tower, Fiona is faced with the truth that her rescuer is not a prince and her true love, but a monster as she says to him, 'This is all wrong, you're not supposed to be an ogre'.

Shrek might not be your typical knight in shining armour, but Fiona is not your typical princess. She can fight, she burps and farts as loud as Shrek does, she is unphased by the creepy and crawly things that dwell in the woods, and she shares a love and fascination for the gross and unconventional things in life. She attributes this to being locked in a tower from a young age, but as the story progresses, we realise that Fiona is hiding something.

If you've been hiding under a rock and have never seen *Shrek* I'm about to spoil it for you; Fiona is cursed and turns into an ogre every night when the sun goes down. The first person to discover this is Donkey. He starts screaming when he catches sight of her, crying, 'Oh my God, you ate the princess'. When she finally gets him to calm down she explains that this double life is her reality until she finds true love. True love's kiss will break the spell and she will 'take love's true form'.

Fiona rails against this curse, calling herself hideous and ugly.

'But Donkey, I'm a princess. And this is not how a princess is supposed to look.'

Right here she exposes, almost accidentally, a fundamental truth about the stories we present to our girls. There is an expectation of femininity and thinness that is to be aspired to. We want our girls to see themselves as leading ladies in their own lives, but we are telling them that they cannot unless they look a certain way.

Fiona is desperate to marry Lord Farquaad, the tyrannical embodiment of small-man-syndrome, who tortures the gingerbread man and skins Momma Bear for a rug for his bedroom (if you have never noticed this before I am sorry to have ruined your innocence), in order to break the spell and remain 'beautiful', even though she has blossoming feelings for Shrek. After the disastrous wedding, when she and Shrek finally admit their feelings for each other and kiss (along with the spectacular transformation scene that parodies the end of *Beauty and the Beast*), Fiona comes out of the magical scene unchanged.

'I don't understand. I'm supposed to be beautiful.'

'But you are beautiful.'

How my heart sang. How I felt validated and seen. When Shrek looks at her like what he is saying is the most obvious thing in the world, I felt so grateful for this film.

Now, with context, I realise that I, and others who look like me and Fiona, were still being called monsters.

I mean, come on! Fiona was cursed to appear as an ogre when the sun goes down, and true love's kiss would break the spell, the spell didn't have any locked-in-a-tower stipulation, that was all her parents' idea. If that was my daughter, I would want to expose them to as many people as possible and teach them about the kindness of love, in the hopes that they would be able to recognise it when it came along. I would not have so much disdain for my child's appearance and be so embarrassed by it that I would lock her in a tower and hope for some chauvinistic asshole, more in love with the idea of saving a woman in need than the woman in question, to go on a suicide mission to rescue her. I don't think the parenting books would approve of that course of action.

Shrek and Fiona get married and go back to live happily ever after in the swamp, but nothing else in the world changes. They are still hunted, hated and despised (as shown in the opening montage of *Shrek 2*) everywhere they go, it just doesn't bother them as much as it used to, because they are happy and together.

While I appreciate this message, is it enough?

When I started dating, I had a type: big, burly men with beards. Men who were the same size or bigger than me. It was a real turn on to feel dainty and small in the arms of someone else, but also it felt safe knowing that there could be no fatphobia directed towards me without extreme hypocrisy. When I look back as an adult (married to a skinny non-binary person), I wonder whether this 'type' I chose was a matter of personal taste or the result of cultural programming. Did I think that I would only find acceptance for my body, find happiness and love, in the arms of a man who lived in a bigger body than mine? Did I find these men attractive because I had written off everyone else as unattainable? Was I so desperate for validation of my body that all it took to sweep me off my feet (figuratively, not literally) was to find me attractive despite society?

Now, big burly men with beards, I love you and will always love you, and you deserve to have flowers in your beards and to be the little spoon at any given time, and this is not me saying that I realised I could do better than you. What I'm saying is that the only thing you 'deserve' in a relationship is love, kindness and compassion, and none of those things are impacted by the way you look, the way your partner looks or the way you look as a couple. Now that I write this it sounds like the most obvious thing in the world, but it really was a shock to me when I realised that I had only really been allowing myself to acknowledge attraction to one kind of demographic. And I'm pansexual! I love everyone! Letting go of the need to feel smaller in my partner's arms because I am a woman allowed me to find the truest love in the most unlikely of places.

Shrek is bigger than Fiona, she is still dainty in his arms. How is it possible that even when we are taking steps forward in progression and representation we still have to follow these set rules and present them to children. Is it any wonder I lusted after men that made me feel small? Was I ever told I could find happiness any other way?

I love the *Shrek* movies. I love the memories I have watching them with my dad, I love that the creators thought the best way to portray an ogre was with a grumpy Scottish man (again drawing parallels with my dad), and I love that they offered me a completely different kind of story to what I was used to.

It taught me that if your body doesn't change, if you do not have a moment of magical transformation, for better or worse, and the way you look is just the way you will always look, that's okay and you still deserve happiness and you are still beautiful.

NON-HUMAN BODIES

Even if you are on the fence about whether Fiona is a positive or negative representation of plus size women in animation, I think we can all agree that she is not a *human* representation.

As someone born in 1990, I would class my developmental years as the 90s and the 00s. Any film and television I took in after that would have been after I started higher education and was taught to think critically about the media I was consuming. Not that I took much of it in, I was a terrible student (I thought Tarantino was the pinnacle of cinema like a right basic bitch), but still, there has been over a decade of animation that has been released into the world since my developmental years.

In the time from the 2010s onwards more plus sized women have cropped up in mainstream animation and film. The issue remains that these characters, such as Mrs Potato Head in *Toy Story*, Gloria the hippo in *Madagascar*, and the Mum and the Manticore characters in *Onward*, have one key thing in common with each other and with Ogre Fiona: they are not in human bodies.

Pixar's 2015 emotional drama *Inside Out* was groundbreaking in its storytelling approach, in its ambition to have its young audiences feel in touch and connected to their emotions, and in its approach to teaching children about mental health. The premise of the story is that we are each governed by five core emotions which operate at a control panel in our brains: Joy, Anger, Fear, Disgust and Sadness. These emotions trigger our memories and help us to respond to situations and help us to navigate life, making core memories that make up the fundamentals of our personality.

The story follows Riley, a pre-teen girl, and her struggle to come to terms with starting a new life when her family moves from the Midwest to San Francisco.

The emotion that is the chief operator in Riley's brain is Joy, a thin, springy character in a nice dress who always tries to keep Riley happy. Joy actively tries to keep Sadness away from having any control over Riley's life.

Sadness is small, plus sized and blue, voiced by the matronly and soft-spoken Phyllis Smith (*The Office*). Side note: Phyllis Smith is an exceptional actress but is only ever cast as 'sad-sack' characters – a wasted talent! The character designers were tasked with creating a character that was the physical embodiment of sadness, and they picked a plus size woman. Although Sadness ends up being the key to Riley processing her essential emotions (teaching the audiences a vital lesson that it's okay to be sad sometimes), and I can appreciate the designers had a challenging task in personifying emotion, the contrast in character design between her and Joy is rather painful.

Something that is not painful though is the 2022 Disney animation *Turning Red*. I absolutely adored this film, in which Chinese Canadian pre-teen protagonist Mei is part of a family where the women are cursed to transform into a giant red panda after they hit puberty (not going to lie, I would have loved that when I was a pre-teen, I absolutely would have mauled my bullies). The panda only comes out when they feel any intense emotion such as stress or anger, which we all know pre-teen girls never do, right?

Having 'The Panda' as a narrative tool to embody the pre-teen experience of rage, fear and intense physical attraction is wonderful, depicting it for what it feels like inside – a beast.

Mei has to learn how to control her emotions in order to use the panda to her best advantage. She uses the stimuli of the love for her female friendships as the grounding memory and thought that allows her to calm down and return to her normal thirteen-year-old body.

All the women in Mei's family refer to their panda as 'my panda', it's personal and individual and something they all chose to have bound, undergoing an intense spiritual ceremony in order to trap the panda's essence in a jade necklace, so it cannot control them anymore.

The suggestion that these women felt that they had to give up a fundamental part of themselves, a part that we have seen be joyful and freeing through Mei's experience, is a powerful comment on the need for women to be palatable and always appealing. It makes me sad that these women felt that their rage and their intense joy (and sexual empowerment? Mei is too young to tell but I get the feeling that the fully-grown panda has all kinds of urges) was something they felt was detrimental to living their lives. I am reminded it was society that was not ready for these women, not the other way around.

Mei's mother's is the biggest enforcer of the ritual and the keenest to have Mei's panda bound, as her own panda is over 100 feet tall and monstrous. When Mei disobeys her mother, abandons the ritual, and goes to a concert instead, her mother's panda breaks free and rampages through the city in search of her daughter. It takes the whole family to bring her down and bind her panda once again.

While the necessity to bind Mei's mother makes me really sad, I loved that in the end Mei chooses to keep her panda, understanding that her emotions do not control her and she does not control them, they work together. Her most intense feelings are where she derives her power from, and her truest sense of self.

My God, I wish I had seen *Turning Red* when I was a young person. To have that kind of validation of my rage and my emotions, after years of being told to 'calm down' would have been a breath of fresh air. To know that my emotions are where I find my power would have changed my life.

There's just one thing; everything Mei goes through as a panda happens to all young women in their regular bodies. In separating the two, and in never showing Mei's heightened emotions in her pre-teen body, that side of her is 'othered'. I have nothing but praise for *Turning Red*, but it is interesting to see that animation is still using the technique of showing women with less 'appealing' attributes (I use that *very* lightly,) in non-human bodies. When will we start seeing these very real female attributes in animated stories grounded in reality?

These characters are strong, powerful and funny, but you have to suspend your disbelief to believe that they are real at all.

Is it easier to swallow a plus size elf or hippo or embodiment of human emotion as a main character in a children's and family film than a plus size human? What if Elsa from *Frozen* was plus size, would she be any less badass and beloved?

BABY STEPS

The world of animation, in which you can make anything move and live, and for an audience who will accept *anything* we place in front of them (kids really are the most progressive of all of us), why is children's animation the slowest medium to champion inclusion?

Disney has a hold on a very particular piece of my heart, and it is the hopeful, sparkly-eyed, arty-farty child part. It pains me to know this company and this corporation, one that has the power to shape the lives of children across the world, is also capable of funding hateful anti-gay legislation in America that actively damaged the lives of queer children. A boardroom full of white men work under the same company banner as the shy and sparkly-eyed actors with pencils who bring these beloved characters to life, but the power discrepancy is clear. However, that's not to say that change isn't coming because of creators standing up to that power.

Thankfully baby steps are being made. In Disney's Oscar-winning 2020 *Encanto*, a film about a gifted, eccentric and eclectic family from a magically-protected region of Colombia, there was no one who spoke to me more than Louisa.

Protagonist Mirabel's oldest sister, Louisa, is gifted with the power of superhuman strength, has the biggest muscles, the biggest heart and the biggest vulnerabilities of the family. Terrified that she is only of worth to her family because of her gift and determined to take on as many family burdens as her strong arms can carry to protect others from pain, Louisa struggles with perfectionism, which she shares with her sister in her song, 'Surface Pressure'. As the family starts losing their powers, no one feels it more than Louisa, who overcompensates to make up for what she thinks she lacks.

Louisa doesn't look like your standard Disney Princess. She is huge with big burly muscles and a face that doesn't fit the standard big-eyed mould of most female Disney characters. She is constantly on the move, knocking down walls and recentring churches, diverting rivers and carrying many donkeys at a time. It makes her vulnerability all the more striking when she admits to her sister that she feels weak and is terrified of losing her gift.

While it is difficult to pinpoint the source of any drama, there were murmurings around the time of the first promo material that showed the character design of Louisa, that the creators faced pressure from executives regarding the design of Louisa's bigger body. Illustrator and character modelling supervisor Dylan Ekren opened up in an interview and explained that Disney were favouring a more classical design for the character of Louisa, but the creative team pushed back and advocated to keep her big and brawny. It made sense for her character to look exactly as she was created.

Because of that push back, we have fan favourite, Louisa, buff and gorgeous and utterly beloved by audiences all over the world. She is unapologetically beautiful and secure in her body, as she states in the lyric that made my heart melt the moment I heard it: 'I move mountains, I move churches, and I glow cause I know what my worth is'.

It is so refreshing to have a character in an alternative body have vulnerabilities that go beyond the physical. I also struggle with perfectionism. During the pandemic some very well-timed therapy helped me to understand that my habit of holding myself to a higher and unattainable standard comes from overcompensating for things from my childhood, from not looking cute and only feeling worthy when being smart or funny. In my youth, I never saw any other women on screen I could relate to going through the same thing.

Louisa's biggest fear is not being useful to her family, feeling she always has to be earning her place. I get that. I wish I had seen this story when I was younger. Instead, all I saw was that it was not okay to be fat. While there's no way for me to tell for sure, I believe a lot less damage would have been done to me, my confidence and my self-worth had I been presented with more of Louisa's story and less of Fiona's.

Louisa is not fat. Not in any way. But she is not thin either. She exists outwith the mould of the traditional female character and therefore she is dangerous to the norm.

Disney is a legacy, and while I understand why that legacy must be protected, we are still fitting the mould of female characters created by designers that laid down the rules in a time when women were still the legal properties of their husbands.

We are taking baby steps in the right direction with characters like Fiona and Louisa, but we can do more. The creative team stood up to the executives and they got to do things their way. *That was brave!* We need to celebrate that bravery and ask these creative teams to continue being brave in the future, championing inclusivity with all their intellectual properties.

Kids are the most progressive group in our society. They don't have any concept of societal norms and pressures, and so they accept what is put in front of them. It is the children of today that will make strides forward in human rights, female autonomy, fighting climate change, LGBTQ+ rights, racism and things that we cannot even begin to imagine. Now is the time that we should be presenting them with a narrative that doesn't call anyone who doesn't look like the heroines of the stories they adore, hideous and ugly.

Ask yourself who was your favourite princess when you were younger. Did you ever dress up like her for Halloween? Which character in animation do you most look like now? Would you ever have dressed up like that character when you were a kid?

My niece is eleven, the same age that I was when I first saw *Shrek*. I cannot look at her and watch movies with her without worrying about their long-term impact. I'm glad she was born and had her developmental years in the times of *She-Ra and the Princesses of Power* and *Turning Red* but she is also a child of social media. There will always be new challenges finding new ways to impact our girls, and as the adults in their lives I hope that we are able to find the language to challenge and call out the unhealthy narratives for what they are, so our girls might learn to do so in turn.

CHAPTER 8

Main Character Energy

As you can tell by now, the FGBF trope is everywhere in film and television, and it doesn't seem to be going anywhere any time soon.

Nonetheless, despite its constant cropping up and its perpetuating of negative stereotypes about plus size women, it hasn't stopped a few shining examples of plus size stories slipping through.

It's time to talk about the ones who made it. The stories that despite all the odds managed to make it to our screens, the ones with plus size women stomping through the story as protagonists with something to say. Women who embody that Main Character Energy I've been searching for.

Take Anne Fletcher's 2018 Netflix original teen film, *Dumplin'*, which is based on a book of the same name. The protagonist, Willowdean Dickson, played by Danielle Macdonald, is a plus size teenager and the daughter of a former Texas beauty queen, played by Jennifer Anniston. Willowdean looks like and takes after her plus size aunt, Lucy, more than her mother. Lucy recently passed away (they allude to her fatness being the part of the reason she died, which is something I'm choosing to not unpack here), and when clearing out her things Willowdean finds a crumpled up half-completed application. It shows that Lucy once thought to enter the Miss Teen Bluebonnet pageant, the competition that Willowdean's mother won as a teenager and still runs to this day. Both inspired by her application form and saddened that Lucy, a woman who radiated self-love and confidence, for some reason didn't go through with it, Willowdean signs up for the pageant for her.

She does so to make a point, challenge her mother and to interrogate the pageant's 'inclusive' policies. In her doing so, she inspires a few other misfits to sign up with her.

As much as Willowdean professes, 'I am not a Joan of Arc for fat girls', she confronts exclusionary practices, speaks out against bias and stands up to bullies who pick on her friends. On her first day of school she gets suspended for kneeing some jerk in the nuts for bullying another plus size girl in her year.

Willowdean joining the pageant is a metaphor for a much bigger act: being seen.

Being part of the pageant circle means being on stage, being looked at by members of your community, being listened to in the interview section, getting to showcase your talents and to stand in a cohort of other young girls that are traditionally considered beautiful. Willowdean is demanding space in this cohort as an equal, and that is what gives her the Main Character Energy. Willowdean, in all manners regarding the pageant, refuses to bow to convention or make herself smaller for the sake of others' comfort or convenience. She marches onto centre stage and steals focus, and she uses heightened drag style makeup and a Dolly Parton backing track to do so. What an icon.

And yet, despite all this, she cannot fathom that the boy she works with has a crush on her.

From the start of the film, Bo, a handsome guy in her work, flirts with her, asks her out, kisses her and then openly tells her he has feelings for her. She reacts badly, turning him down even though she really likes him: 'You and I, we don't work in the real-world Bo. You're supposed to be with someone like Becca'. She gestures to her body and asks him how he doesn't see the problem.

Willowdean is willing to take on the oppressive and exclusionary practices of the pageant circles of Texas, demanding her place in the competition because she is just as good and deserving as everyone else, proclaiming that a 'swimsuit body' is nothing more than a body with a swimsuit on it, but when it comes to romantic love that literally presents itself on a plate to her, she rejects it because she feels unworthy.

This once again reinforces the narrative that the body can be an obstacle to romantic love. And that plus size girls and women are expected to be passed over, ignored, even ridiculed when it comes to romance, and to expect to be rejected at every turn. Because Willowdean is challenging the social norms within the pageant circle, the creators are telling the audience that this is something that can be changed, and maybe Willowdean is the person strong enough to change it.

When Willowdean acknowledges the problems that would come from her and Bo being together, not just between the two of them but how the rest of their community would view their relationship, and how Bo would suffer and be ridiculed for being involved with a fat girl, the creators are telling the audience that this is something that cannot be changed.

Bo is absent from this point until the end of the film. Willowdean progresses with the pageant, enlists the help of some local drag queens who were friends of her aunt Lucy and dazzles along with her friends. She is disqualified on a technicality, but the whole process brings her and her mother closer, and the two see their worth outwith the boundaries of the pageant. Moreover, one of Willowdean's friends, Millie, another plus size girl with a sunny disposition and a determination to stay kind and positive (everything about her just screams beauty queen) comes in second place. She loses to the tiny blonde frontrunner, but it's still a victory for fat girls everywhere.

High off her personal victory at the pageant, and with a renewed sense of self-worth, Willowdean seeks out Bo and accepts his love. It is a beautiful scene that is understated and honest, and it works hard to spell out that the only thing standing in Willowdean's way to have the relationship she and Bo both craved, was her sense of self.

Don't get me wrong, it's really lovely to see Willowdean get to a place where she knows that she is worthy and nothing can stand in her way, but I have seen the 'fat girl gets the guy after she self-flagellates and acknowledges that she doesn't deserve the guy' narrative played out before. It reminds me of Jo Brand's comedy set: Jo needs to address the elephant in the room by laughing at herself before others will laugh with her, and Willowdean has to acknowledge that she shouldn't have love because she is fat before she is given love.

Dumplin' is a feel good, confidence-inspiring film that is a joy to watch every time, and Macdonald's turn in the lead role is fresh and joyful, I wish I could do nothing but praise it, but this does niggle me. Macdonald's other roles have all been wonderfully detached from the FGBF stereotypes, her turn as a hopeful pregnant woman in a post-apocalyptic world in *Bird Box*, and her turn as a sexual assault survivor trying to make sense of her new normal in *Unbelievable* were both nuanced, powerful and heart-breaking. She is a force to be reckoned with and she has continued her Leading Lady streak in *Falling for Figaro*. Going back and watching *Dumplin'* after seeing Macdonald's career progress so beautifully I can't help but feel that niggle for what could have been pretty perfect.

In no other romantic comedy is the main character required to make a statement of unworthiness in order to get the guy. I mean, there are exceptions to the rule. See Clementine in *Eternal Sunshine of the Spotless Mind* telling Joel that she's just a fucked-up girl looking for her own piece of mind. However, the difference between the alt-girl pushing away the geeky guy isn't to save him from the embarrassment of being with her, it's to make sure he knows that she is a fully-formed person and not just an exciting concept (yes, in case I haven't been explicit enough, I am talking about the Manic Pixie Dream Girl trope. *Urgh!*). Clementine is telling Joel she is a fully-formed human being and that might disappoint him. Willowdean is telling Bo she's not worthy of being considered as a fully-formed human being, because she is fat.

When Bo tells Willowdean, 'I think you're beautiful, and to hell with anyone who even made you feel otherwise', my heart fluttered. Bo realises that Willowdean's hesitance doesn't come from the personality he is attracted to, but from years of being conditioned to think less of herself.

I hate that this is a thing, but it's kind of true. We are conditioned to think less of ourselves. To move away from what we want to put the comfort of others first, to acknowledge our very bodies as an inconvenience. We don't want to be an inconvenience.

Bringing back *Schitts Creek* for a moment, could fiction ever take a leaf out of the Canadian sitcom's book and place the romance in a world without fatphobia? Would the characters still have as much drive to be together without the conflict of living in a fatphobic society that would deem their relationship unbalanced and odd?

Part of me wishes we had more time with Willowdean and Bo on screen, because I feel that seeing that relationship overcome that hurdle would be very interesting and honest and not shown on screen before; however, it's not Bo's story, it's Willowdean's. And Willowdean was making waves at the pageant which had no time for her boy drama, so it's good that Bo is not there.

The work that Willowdean must do takes time and is hard, and *Dumplin'* isn't a relationship narrative.

SEX AND MY MAD FAT DIARY

Love is a strong motivator in any story; as women we are conditioned to look up to princesses and wait for Prince Charming. It's no surprise that the genre of film that has the most female protagonists is the romantic comedy (and the horror genre, I'm sure there's something worth unpacking in that). I'm a sucker for romance, I love a good love story, and there's nothing more magical than a first on screen kiss.

But what about sex?

As I've mentioned before, we as audiences subconsciously understand cinematic language as a way to pick up on silent cues and hints about the story and characters. For example, if a character has a cough, it's a signifier that they are seriously ill (think Nicole Kidman in *Moulin Rouge*). Any dying character on screen will always have a cough. If a character has glasses, we understand them to be intelligent, maybe even 'geeky' (like Velma in *Scooby Doo*).

When we see an adult kiss on screen, we understand it signifies a relationship and has connotations of sex.

Sex is a difficult thing to capture regarding a plus size main character. Along with the plethora of emotions that come with engaging with a new sexual partner for the first time – the excitement, anticipation and insecurity – with a plus size character we understand there is a background of cultural oppression and a varying history of dysmorphia surrounding their body.

With the rise of high-end productions employing the services of intimacy coordinators, people whose jobs it is to work with the actors and director to create a pre-planned and rehearsed series of actions to depict sex on screen, and who create a safe environment for the actors on set, sex scenes in drama are also on the rise. Scenes that are being depicted in ways that are intimate and beautiful, grounded in reality and not through the lens of the male gaze. You just have to look at series one of *Bridgerton* to see the impact that proper intimacy coordination can have on a production and how sex can steer a story.

While this offers a new and exciting way to explore on screen romance, I have yet to see this fully taken advantage of when using a plus size character. I have high hopes for *Bridgerton* Season Three, where the central romantic figures will be Colin Bridgerton and Penelope Featherington, played by the rising star Nicola Coughlan, whose character is the one often overlooked and ignored by society. I'm not holding my breath though. There's a million ways not to show a fat girl fuck.

It's not entirely surprising that we haven't seen more explicit and coordinated intimacy scenes with plus size actresses, it's still relatively new in mainstream media. Yet, when plus size characters tie their worthiness of having a romantic storyline to their bodies it leaves no room for any expression of sexual desire.

When I was a teenager I felt lucky if anyone fancied me. Like I didn't deserve it, and that this person must be someone of strong character if they were bucking society and looking past the obvious defect of my size in order to like me. This thinking made any romantic attachment on my end centre around my partner's desire; what encouraged it, how I could keep it and how to make myself as small as possible as to not accidentally do something fat and make them stop fancying me. It was all about them.

I was a downright thirsty teenager. It's amazing to me now that I can look back on that time and know that my desires (which were like my hormones; absolutely rampant) were completely overlooked when it came to romantic attachment.

Channel 4's 00s hit show *My Mad Fat Diary*, based on the real diaries of writer and comedian, Rae Earl, are a triumph of teenage sexuality.

The story follows Rae, a seventeen-year-old, plus size girl living in Lincolnshire played by Sharon Rooney, as she navigates college, new friendships and relationships, and her boy-crazy and sexually explicit inner monologue. Having just been released from a psychiatric institute where she spent time getting support with her mental health and eating disorder, she goes through the summer tentatively. She attends weekly counselling sessions with the grouchy Dr Kester and visits her friend, Tix, who is not well enough to leave the hospital.

My Mad Fat Diary deals with heavy subjects and it doesn't shy away from the brutal truth of mental health and eating disorders. While this could be the main focus on the story, the show presents itself more as a comedy, and that's because of Rae.

Rae is a fully-fledged character who is going through mental anguish, but that's only one part of her life. She also has intrusive and hilarious thoughts about boys and sex and all the things she could be doing with boys, *like having sex.*

Sex can be overpowering at any stage in a young adult or adult's life, for those who feel sexual desire it will be most likely be a force that takes up a lot of brain space, and what *My Mad Fat Diary* does is give it the space it deserves on screen.

What makes Rae different as a character is the fact that she is so honest in her inner monologue, that any sort of self-flagellation for her size and feelings of being undeserving of romance, which do happen, don't touch her sexual desire. The fact that she is shown to have sexual desire and sexual autonomy is the biggest strength of the show, as it shows that even though as fat women we are aware of how we should be feeling about our bodies and how we are expected to navigate the landscape of sexual relationships, we are normal when it comes to our wants, desires and thoughts. We are not exempt from these feelings just because we are told we should be. We, even when we are in the absolute depths of struggle regarding our relationship with our bodies, are still beings that have extremities and emotions that are contradictory to our journeys.

What's more, Rae gets to explore her sexual desires on camera in a consensual, healthy and loving relationship with her boyfriend, Finn. She repeatedly deals with the negative voices and the punishing internal monologue, her feelings of unworthiness even causing them to break up at one point but even though she acknowledges those thoughts and learns how to overcome them. It's such an important, sad and beautiful journey to see played out on screen. Her partner is unwavering in his support for her but she makes it clear that she needs to address and unpack her feelings towards herself. His positive comments and attitude are not enough.

I would find it so much easier to swallow the FGBF trope if, even just for a second, we got to see a fraction of the honesty and humanity we are shown with Rae.

Unpicking the cinematic language that dictates that on screen sex is equivalent to loose morals and 'whorish' tendencies is never more powerfully depicted when the sexual relations shown are tender, consensual, enthusiastic and explorative.

Maybe it's just me, but there's nothing I can relate more to than being boy crazy. And girl crazy. And sex crazy. Getting to see that unflinchingly articulated on screen made me feel like my secret blushing thoughts were valid, which had never happened up until that point.

I wish there were more examples that I could explore, more highlights of plus size actors getting to be part of beautiful and cinematic love scenes that are tender and romantic (and not in any way played for laughs), but there are tragically few. Apart from rare examples, such as Big Boo and her lover in a flashback scene in *Orange is the New Black*, or Becky Williams engaging in a gorgeous and steamy love scene on a New York rooftop in *Empire* (both of which I had to *hunt* for) it's clear we have a long way to go in representing sexuality on screen for plus size characters.

As the incomparable Oscar nominated actress, Gabourey Sidibe, who played Becky Williams in *Empire* said in interviews after her sex scene aired, 'There's never been someone of my skin colour, my size, with somebody of the same skin colour in a love scene on primetime television'.

THIN GIRL BEST FRIEND

Seeing more and more plus size women smashing it in leading roles in film and television gives me hope that the FGBF trope might finally be on the out.

Maybe every time a new plus size best friend character is written and brought to life on our screens, she will have more and more character development and wants of her own that don't rely on the success of the Thin Lead. A purpose that goes beyond cheering on her Thin Lead, and a sense of self-worth that allows her to challenge her best friend whenever she feels used, neglected or overlooked.

But, with the rise of plus size women claiming their lead narratives in their own films and television shows, what about *their* best friends? Does the Fat Girl Lead have a FGBF? Is there such a trope as the Thin Girl Best Friend?

While I love Willowdean and Rae, their characters and their worlds, both of their stories have a driving force, an engine if you will, that is powered by their weight. So many of their decisions and developments stem directly from their relationships with their bodies, and how they feel disadvantaged socially because of their bodies. In both *Dumplin'* and *My Mad Fat Diary*, the main characters have to come to terms with their weight and find confidence despite this. As someone who has had similar struggles, I understand the reality of your weight being a factor in all of your decisions, but when it came to my confidence I always had friends I could rely on for support when I felt lacking in that department. While we know exactly what the role of a FGBF is, are the expectations the same when the roles are reversed and a plus size woman is in the lead role and her Thin Friend is the supporting character?

Look at the role of Chloe, as played by Jodie Comer, in *My Mad Fat Diary*. Chloe is ambitious, beautiful, privileged and she is completely oblivious to Rae's struggles with her body confidence and mental health. To Chloe, social hierarchy is very important, and being admired by boys is something she makes synonymous with her self-worth. She can afford to because she is admired wherever she goes.

What I found interesting about Chloe is that while she is always there to chime in her opinions and insight when it comes to Rae's journey, as all best friends do, Chloe's commentary almost serves as the voice of society, reminding Rae of all the reasons that she shouldn't be confident. She actively discourages Rae from speaking about her mental health and telling her friend group about her time in an institution. She does really unhealthy things around Rae, like taking up smoking in order to lose weight even though she's about a UK Size 6 (which I know doesn't have any bearing on confidence, weight insecurities and eating disorders can afflict people of any size) and doesn't even acknowledge that her vocalisation of being the size she is and needing to lose weight makes her negative opinions on Rae's weight heard loud and clear. Chloe constantly tries to use peer pressure and other societal forms of manipulation as ways to control Rae.

It makes me think that while the FGBF trope is there to set the Thin Lead free, the Thin Girl Best Friend trope is there to keep the Fat Girl Main Character contained.

When we look at the relationship between Monica and Rachel in *Friends*, specifically their relationship during the many iterations of Fat Monica, Rachel acts superior to Monica because of her extensive life experience. She is the authority on all things because, as a fat person, Monica is excluded from society so has had no opportunity to gain any life experience of her own. It's almost exclusively about relationships, but whenever Monica is fat, Rachel gives out the most obvious advice as if Monica is completely clueless. Their friendship is very one-sided whenever Monica is in the fat suit, however their friendship is very much equal when Monica is thin, sometimes Monica even has the upper hand being a more worldly person living in the city and being a lot less privileged than Rachel.

When Monica loses the weight, Rachel rewards her with respect. Rewards her by viewing her as on her level socially, and so competition for her in life and in love.

Monica and Rachel have their ups and downs throughout the series, but they stand as competition against each other on more than one occasion. That would never happen if Monica had been fat the whole time because Rachel or indeed anyone else would not have seen her as a threat.

While I am absolutely delighted to be seeing more plus size women in leading roles it baffles me that their best friend counterparts, characters who surely have seen their struggles and while maybe not being able to fully understand, they would certainly be able to empathise, are written in such a way that they police the confidence of their best friend. In a way, this takes all the cruelty that fat people deal with daily and gives it a face and voice that should be friendly and comforting. In doing so the creators are almost justifying this treatment, boiling the negative stereotypes down to a 'sad but true' shoulder shrug of a stance, deeming it acceptable.

After all, we condone the behaviour we ignore, and if we have a fat main character accepting this negativity from their best friend and ignoring any subtle fatphobia because it's presented in a familiar way, it's condoned loud and clear.

'I NEVER SAW YOU AS FAT'

There was a moment in *Dumplin'* that lives rent-free in my head. It's when Willowdean breaks away from her best friend Elle because she is feeling insecure that Elle is fitting in with all the other beautiful, thin girls at the pageant. Elle has a whole other social landscape that Willowdean feels she cannot be part of, as Elle works in a High Street retail store that doesn't carry plus size clothing. Because of this, Elle has a number of work colleagues that are also thin and also in the pageant. Willowdean feels like she is no longer in the pageant as her own agent, there with an agenda, she feels like she is standing on the outside of Elle's cool friendship group and it makes her feel small. She asks Elle to quit, arguing that Elle could never understand what Willowdean is going through and why she decided to sign up. When Elle leaves upset, Willowdean shouts after her to go join her colleagues at 'the store that hates fat people'.

Elle marches back, tearful, and says, 'For your information, Willowdean, I never saw you as fat'.

I understand what Elle is saying. I understand that she is trying to tell Willowdean that the way she looks has never once impacted how Elle thinks or feels about her best friend. I know it is meant to be a sign of support and love, but it's a little misguided.

Elle's not blind. Willowdean is fat.

When Willowdean uses the word 'fat' to describe herself she means it in the connotative sense of the word; ugly and unlovable. When

Elle says she never saw Willowdean as fat, she means she never saw her as ugly or unlovable.

But she doesn't *say* that. She says 'fat'.

Elle is trying to tell Willowdean that she has never considered her best friend's weight to have any negative connotations, but the sheer fact that she is using the descriptive word 'fat' to convey a social construct belies that fact.

I cannot begin to count the number of times I have called myself fat in a self-deprecating way, and then felt the warm glow of approval when a friend in the vicinity assured me I was not fat. What gorgeous lies.

I am fat. There. I'm saying it. This is my moment of reclamation.

I need to let go of the social connotations and my negative personal history with the word in order to describe my amazing body in a way that doesn't make me feel lesser than anyone else. I'm fat. I also have blue eyes. I'm not tall but not short either. My hair is red, but it's dyed, it's been so long since I saw my natural colour I'm actually not sure what it is anymore. I'm all these things, and I'm also fat.

There's nothing wrong with that. It doesn't say anything about my personality, my habits or my worth. It doesn't mean I cannot do physical activity and it doesn't mean I am less likely to find love. It does not mean that people get to treat me badly, exclude me or judge me. It doesn't mean I need to make myself smaller for the comfort of others.

I didn't always believe that though.

Maybe what would have been better for me when I was younger, a teenager or even in my early twenties, was to be called out for fishing for pleasing lies when calling myself fat.

Someone should have said to me, 'Yes, you are. So fucking what?'

Now, if I had heard that when I was a teenager I would have gone into a foul mood that would have lasted days, but I would have known not to try and pull that compliment-fishing self-deprecating act (and by that I mean bullshit) again around that particular friend, which would have drummed some perspective into me.

I am trying to reconcile all this, but it is a process. A journey. And there is no rush. It's my choice. However, I know that it would be easier for me to reclaim the word fat if I saw more people doing the same publicly.

There's no cliché I hate more in film and television than when a thin woman approaches her male partner and asks, 'Does this [whatever] make me look fat?'

This phrase is always portrayed as a trap for the man, as there is apparently no right answer to this question. The straight up answer of 'no' suggests that there are things that can make someone look fat, and that their partner is open to interpretations of fatness. Any hesitation is taken as looking for confirmation of possible fatness, which is also an insult to the thin woman, who is horrified at the possibility of ever being perceived as fat, even though she posed the question in the first place.

As I've mentioned before, clothes are not magic mirrors. Maybe we should stop asking stupid questions and start just telling the truth. Maybe there's something a little badass about that.

GETTING IT RIGHT WITH *JUST WRIGHT*

I thought I knew every rom-com to have come out of Hollywood over the past twenty years, but one passed me by that I only discovered in researching this book, and I am very sad to have only just discovered now.

The 2010 film, *Just Wright*, directed by Sanaa Hamri and starring Queen Latifah and Common in the leading roles, is a part romantic comedy, part underdog sports film that is fresh and charming and full of love.

Latifah plays Leslie Wright, a top physiotherapist and die-hard basketball fan (specifically the New Jersey NETS). She is unlucky in love, as everyone she dates sees her as good friend material and not girlfriend material. A chance meeting at a gas station introduces her to one of her heroes, star player Scott McKnight. The pair hit it off immediately and he invites her to his birthday party. Leslie goes and invites her old friend and godsister Morgan, who looks like a supermodel and aspires to being a trophy wife. Before Leslie and

Scott can advance their friendship, Morgan, through manipulative tactics, catches Scott's attention, and the pair end up dating and then getting engaged. Sometime after that, Scott tears his posterior cruciate ligament in a game and his career is put on the line. Not trusting Scott's blonde and leggy physiotherapist, Morgan gives Leslie the job, not seeing her as a threat of any kind. When it looks like Scott's career might be over, Morgan leaves him to chase another star. Leslie stays and helps Scott to recovery, their time together showing them both how compatible they are, and they fall in love in the process.

It is worth saying here that in this film it is questionable whether you can call Queen Latifah plus size. She lives in a bigger body and she is by no means entertainment thin, but she straddles the line a bit. I think it is still important to mention her and this film here because the character of Leslie is always praised for being smart, funny and beautiful, but she is passed over by men and seen as just a friend and not a romantic interest. The film is making a comment that no matter the personal connection and shining personality of the woman, if she is not entertainment thin and has the look of someone who fell out of a magazine, she is not as desirable. Leslie embraces her femininity, wearing dresses on dates and to Scott's party and she also embraces the colours of her team when she's at the game. She is a woman with multitudes, and unlike Morgan, she can be more than one thing at any given time. Morgan wants to be a trophy wife, and so she always lives like a trophy wife. Leslie would be more likely to fix a twinge in an arm rather than sit on it like a prize.

The fact that Leslie works in sports is also an amazingly progressive step for a character in a bigger body. Leslie is never perceived to be unhealthy or slovenly, she is the healthiest person in the film. She is an elite athlete trainer, a professional working in sports, it's refreshing to see someone who looks like her be an authority in that world.

The strongest part of *Just Wright* is how Leslie is always true to herself. She will not play games to get a man, shy away from her unfeminine side, diminish herself professionally in a male-dominated sporting world or accept anything except what she deserves, which is true and long-lasting love.

Leslie and Scott's romance is a tentative and lovely thing. It's clear the two hit it off when they first met, and they probably would have ended up together quicker if Morgan hadn't set her sights on Scott. After Morgan's departure and Leslie and Scott spend more time together alone, the film hits all the romantic beats that grace all the great rom-coms. I mean, Leslie even gets a descending down the staircase in a ballgown for God's sake! And they get together with a romantic kiss and the suggestion of a sex scene, and the following morning she dances like a goofball in the sheets, upper arms and bear shoulders out for the world to see.

When Morgan comes back after Scott makes a full recovery and returns to the life of a star MBA player, Leslie removes herself from the situation. Morgan lies about her reasons for returning, and Leslie sees Scott fall for it because he wants to believe it. She does not ask him to choose her and she does not back away because she bows out before the Thin Girl Best Friend. She leaves because she knows that she deserves Scott to choose her, no questions asked.

What I find amazing about *Just Wright* is that even though in multiple occasions Leslie is treated by others as a FGBF, she never, not even for a second, lets that inform the way she thinks and feels about herself. Leslie is the main character in her own story, and she goes through her life knowing her worth and demanding that people who want to be in her life acknowledge that and treat her accordingly.

She never tears down Morgan, exposing her for being fake, even when she has every opportunity. She is never anything but happy for Morgan when things go her way.

When he finally realises that what he has with Morgan is completely superficial compared to what he had with Leslie, Scott comes to find her to profess his love for her. Leslie refuses to let herself settle for anything except first place. Even though she (and the film) acknowledges that the Morgans of the world are more greatly desired and rewarded for just looking like they fell off the cover of a magazine, Leslie does not make allowances for that when it comes to her love story. Doesn't matter that she is not Morgan, she is still the goddamn protagonist and deserves a happy ending fitting of one.

Leslie Wright is the rom-com heroine I have been waiting for. She places the utmost value on who she is and what she puts out into the world, and is rewarded for her authenticity, her steadfastness, her humour and her heart. We all deserve more Leslies on our screen.

ORANGE IS THE NEW BLACK: AN ODE TO THE ENSEMBLE CAST

It was only a matter of time before I wrote a book, it's impossible to get me to shut up. I was born with the gift of the gab and, God, do I like to use it. There's just so much to talk about! Sadly, it's just not possible to talk about, talk fully on or give space to everything you want to discuss at length. There's only so much geeking out about any given subject you can do on any given day.

That's exactly how I feel about all the women I have mentioned in this book. It has been wonderful to deep dive into so many films, television programmes and properties over the course of the previous sections, but I feel I need to give a mention to all the incredible women I have missed out on, and no group of properties has been neglected more than the ensemble cast.

Narrowing the focus to the main character and best friend dynamics in film and television has meant that characters like Miranda Bailey in *Grey's Anatomy*, Phyllis in *The Office*, Donna in *Parks and Recreation*, Miss Patty in *Gilmore Girls,* Penelope Featherington in *Bridgerton*, Kat in *Euphoria*, Viv in *Sex Education* and so many more have not been given space in this work. I could have written chapters upon chapters about their greatness and the way they strengthen their stories.

However, I could not bring this work to a close without mentioning the shining example for body positive representation on screen; *Orange is the New Black.*

Netflix's gritty, nuanced and powerful drama set in the Litchfield Women's Correctional Center initially follows the story of Piper, a privileged white woman serving a sentence for aiding her drug smuggling ex-girlfriend in taking drug money across borders. While you could argue that Piper is the main character, almost as soon as she enters the prison the scope of the story widens to include an ensemble cast of women from every background imaginable. Piper is the vehicle that allows the stories of the other women to be shown.

While Piper thinks she will stand out from these women, as she believes she is not a typical criminal, she soon realises that she is no different from every other woman in there: she is a human being with wants and needs and a history, a person who is trying her hardest just to survive a horribly trying period of her life.

Over the seven seasons of the show there have been more than 30 characters that you could name as a 'main character', all of them having Main Character Energy, their arcs and development taking up space and having real impact on the story. The show is fearless in its approach to casting, bringing to light characters of all ethnicities, body types, socioeconomic backgrounds and sexualities.

Danielle Brook's portrayal of the larger-than-life Tasha 'Taystee' Jefferson propelled her to the status of fan favourite within only a few episodes. Taystee goes through so much over the course of the show, reaching heights at the centre of a beloved community and friendship circle, to the absolute pits of losing her best friend to police brutality and being framed for the murder of a prison guard.

This would normally be the part where I dive into the relationship between the character, her body and the story, but in this case I have absolutely nothing to say. Taystee's bigger body never once has any impact on her story or development. She is unapologetically herself all the way along; funny, smart, beautiful and fearless. Everything that she goes through, the complete spectrum of human emotion perfectly articulated by Brooks, she reacts to with Main Character Energy, because in her world she is the main character.

And this isn't the only occasion *Orange is the New Black* smashes it out of the park. Taystee is my favourite character, and that's because I relate to her character and the way she walks through the world. But there are so many other characters, all plus size, who have incredible arcs and storylines and multi-season developments that have absolutely no mention of the character's weight.

Black Cindy, in what starts as a scheme to try and get the kosher meal option in the canteen, goes on a journey of spiritual discovery that leads her to converting to Judaism and changing her name to Tova.

Red, after spending a long time locked up in solitary confinement in the final series, struggles with symptoms of dementia, and tries to keep herself together and present as the matronly figure the women around her have always known her to be, even though they are the first to notice the changes in her behaviour.

Big Boo takes her sexuality into her own hands (pun absolutely intended) by fashioning a dildo out of a stolen screwdriver! What a legend.

Orange is the New Black has never once shied away from the brutal reality of life in and after prison for these women. The story does not end well for Taystee, and it broke my heart. She never got a happy ending but neither do so many incarcerated women. At every turn the show remains a pillar of reality, championing women of all backgrounds, sizes, ages and sexual orientations, and their experiences behind bars. I could spend pages and pages highlighting all the ways that this piece is a breakthrough feminist property.

But I can't because that's not the book I'm writing now. What I mean is that there is no point in me saying everything that is worth saying about *Orange is the New Black*, because this is a book about the representation of plus size women in film and television, and there's nothing more to say than *Orange is the New Black* handles this representation in one essential way: *faithfully*.

It's not a bad thing that I can't find much to say on this subject in the seven seasons of the show. On the contrary, it's a very good thing. But of all the ensemble casts that didn't make their way into these chapters, *Orange is the New Black* and my girl Taystee, is one I couldn't let go by unmentioned.

Taystee never acts like she is playing the role of a best friend or a less worthy subordinate. She reacts like she is the main character of her own life. That shouldn't be as shocking to us as it is.

Taystee's Main Character Energy sits within a cast of over 40 women, all with their own Main Character Energy. Perfection. It's all I could ask for. It's everything I aspire to in my writing and in my life.

IT'S ALL ABOUT CHANGING THE WORLD

It's all about the ending.

When we follow a fat girl character on a narrative journey, the question we must ask ourselves in the end is, 'Has the world really changed?

When I got my place at university, in my first Film and Media lecture we learned the basics of storytelling, how all stories follow similar narratives and how all main characters go on their own kind of quest. This is colloquially known as *The Hero's Journey*.

Joseph Campbell's *Hero with a Thousand Faces* is a seventeen-act narrative structure that is used to explain the fundamentals of all stories. The Hero's journey is seen time and time again throughout film and television, some classic examples that follow it very obviously are *The Lion King*, *Harry Potter and the Philosopher's Stone*, *The Matrix*, *The Hobbit* and *Star Wars*, it's easy to spot once you know about it (if this concept is new to you I recommend falling down a YouTube hole of video essays on the subject, it really is fascinating).

The seventeen stages can be simplified into three acts: 'The Ordinary World', 'The Supernatural World' and 'The Return'. Basically, our protagonist starts in a routine that either by circumstance, accident or necessity, they are forced out of. They go on a journey that is full of trials and challenges, meeting with mentors and reconciling with parents and gods, and it all builds to a moment of climax in which the character needs to acknowledge a fundamental change within themselves in order to defeat the evil and receive the rewards. They then return to the Ordinary World, but it has changed somehow because of their actions. Harry Potter defeats Quirrell and Voldemort, Luke Skywalker blows up the Death Star and defeats the Empire, Simba becomes king of Pride Rock.

Now, there is a lot of scholarly conversation about the role of women within the hero's journey (note, they are rarely the hero, sigh!), but what I have noticed is that when the hero is a plus size woman, often at the end of the journey she is changed but the world has not, which is very unsatisfying to me. Patty in *Insatiable* doesn't want to change the world that has been historically cruel to her when she was living in a bigger body, she wants to destroy it from the inside by getting the crown, denying the others who bullied her from getting it. It's petty and vain and does nothing to change the world, and it takes a strange dark turn when Patty becomes a serial killer (don't ask), suggesting that her time as a fat girl damaged her so much that she is only now able to express her homicidal tendencies as a thin person. Sigh again!

Think of Shrek and Fiona. The wedding at the end of the film, on their swamp together surrounded by friends and fairy-tale creatures as everyone belts out the Smash Mouth classic, 'I'm a Believer', and they ride away into the sunset in a carriage shaped like an onion, happily ever after. However, they are still in their swamp. Still in exile. At the start of *Shrek 2* we see a montage of their honeymoon, and while they whimsically run towards each other through a field in slow motion, they are pursued on both sides by mobs of villagers with torches and pitchforks. While the two don't seem to take any heed of the mob, it's clear that the attitudes towards ogres has not changed, even after Shrek's heroics in the first film. If the world was changed, they would be living in their swamp but acknowledged as members of their society and not still living as happy outcasts.

It's a small thing, but it is really important for fat women to know that their stories can change the world too.

Hoping for happiness in a place that has oppressed us is not enough. We are allowed to demand more from the world that we live in. Our Main Character Energy might come from the fact that we demand more.

Willowdean opened the door to the pageant world. I have no idea what I'm doing most of the time, but I know that I want to hold the door open for others like me and stories like mine. I want to demand more. And while I know that my life is real and the stories mentioned here are not, I need to stop hoping for a happy ending. I need to stop waiting for an inciting incident to set me off on my hero's journey to be a main character. I've just got to live. I've just got to live with myself. And I've got to be happy.

The thing is: confidence is hard. When you're a woman growing up being faced with a media and a society that is so focused on the aesthetic, the personal brand, that puts such high value on thinness, it is so hard to feel confident and happy in yourself. It's hard for everyone, not just plus size women.

Imagine your confidence as a scale between 0 and a 100. If you have no confidence within yourself, you sit at a zero. If you are That Bitch every moment of your life, you sit at 100.

That scale is sliding and it can change every day, but what thin people do not understand is that fat people don't start at zero, we start at minus twenty.

Not only do we have to find confidence in ourselves, but we also have to find it in the face of being told by the media and society that we actively should not be confident, we should be ashamed of ourselves and our bodies. We have an external force bringing down our confidence just for being.

So, even on a good day, plus size women need to find twenty points of confidence within themselves just to start at the same level as everyone else. They have to do some daily unpicking of negative narratives before they can start to feel good.

Confidence is something to aspire to, and it is so much easier when you have role models to look up to.

Representation is everything. If you can see it you can be it. It's why I am so happy to see the women mentioned in this chapter doing amazing things and know that I can do amazing things too. More women living their life out loud, confident and authentic, really happy, might cause the numbers to eventually shift. Maybe in five to ten years' time, the confidence of plus size women might start at minus ten as opposed to minus twenty. It's not perfect but it's a start. The less work we have to do to make ourselves feel worthy of the limelight the better. And all I can do, all anyone can do, is hold the door open.

This journey can be lonely. It can be hard to keep going when you feel that the world is against you. And while I acknowledge I am very privileged to be in a position where I am able to work in film and television and write a book like this in the first place, I am under no illusions that the world is against me.

I am working-class, plus size, queer and a woman; these inter-sections cause me daily challenges that I have to overcome, and I know I am not alone in this. The thing that has helped me face these challenges is confidence.

I claim my space unapologetically and demand more. It takes confidence.

The confidence I have is not genetic, it is not an intrinsic part of me tied to my personality. It is something that is nurtured and attended to and grown. It is so healthy because at every stage in my life I am bolstered by the incredible female friends in my life.

Female friendship is everything. It's the reason there are so many stories that carry the message that the love of a best friend can be just as important, life altering and fulfilling as romantic love.

Friends who see your struggle and support. Who see your size and don't flinch. Who treat you as an equal in every way.

I really believe that female friendship is the *silver bullet* that could finally kill the FGBF trope dead.

CHAPTER 10
Female Friendship is the Silver Bullet

God knows, the world has changed a lot over the past few years.

Advocacy in every marginalised community pushes forward with new waves of determination and bravery. Despite the political landscape at home and abroad, progression is not something you can easily stifle and there is nothing in better service of progression than art.

Art and stories stand in the face of all bleak hopelessness, reach for understanding and pull us out of the darkness. Darkness is something we can all relate to. Everyone has gone through darkness in some form of another and come out of the other side, most of the time with a little help.

While I have many institutions, people and stories that have helped me personally escape my own darkness, there's not a wider umbrella term to encapsulate the thing that time and time again saves me from the darkness than female friendship.

From before my memory was fully formed right up until today, the importance of female friendship has been a cultural teaching, an institution, a lifeline that has never let me down. I would not be writing this without it.

In case you haven't picked up my subtle complaining from the previous God knows how many pages, our society fucking sucks. Women are pitted against each other, trained to compete for every opportunity and to feel a sense of social dominance when tearing down other women. It's a sick and tired teaching, and it's so ingrained it's hard to unpick, but our society doesn't *just* tell we women to hate each other. That same society teaches girls to go to the bathroom in groups. It teaches them to text each other when they get home at night. And it teaches them that there's no problem that can't be solved with a good cry, a cuddle, some ice cream and a chick flick. Womxn and gender marginalised people have a hard time just existing in this environment, never mind those trying to thrive.

Female friendship is a power that saved me and continues to save me as I make my way in this industry and in this life. There's nothing I find more joyful than seeing this power and this love and these stories accurately represented on screen.

And when one of the friends looks like me it's a hefty bonus.

2020 saw the release of Olivia Wilde's directorial debut: the coming-of-age comedy set the night before a High School graduation, *Booksmart*.

High School seniors Molly and Amy are academic overachievers and feminist activists – I loved them the moment I saw them. I related so hard.

Amy, the shy, queer and quiet adventurer, played by Kaitlyn Denver, prepares for a gap year in Cambodia before starting college and struggles with how to tell her best friend they will be on different academic timelines for the first time in their lives. Molly, the valedictorian overachiever and class president, played by the powerhouse of comedy, Beanie Feldstein, looks forward to escaping the banality of High School and going to a place where she believes she will thrive as an intellectual, activist and political voice, Yale University.

The premise of the film is that these two girls have spent their High School years slaving away academically while ignoring all social experiences of regular High Schoolers, all in order to get into a top college. They get a very rude awakening when they realise a lot of their classmates, people who squeezed the life out of everything High School society had to offer, also got into the top schools. They feel like they wasted a lot of time not having fun, but they have one night to have such a blow out that it makes up for their years of self-sacrificing.

If this were any other American High School movie, Molly and Amy would have been immediately shown to be bullied and pitied outcasts. As I have mentioned many times when talking about other films in this genre, the social hierarchy that is intrinsically implied is such an overused tool for quickly establishing character and situation that it is used as a crutch to prop up lazy scripts. Wilde's decision to deviate away from this depiction of High School and instead show Molly and Amy as tolerated – maybe not beloved but certainly accepted – members of the Student Body was delightfully refreshing. The first time I watched it I was holding my breath waiting for the moment when Molly gets her lunch tray slapped out of her hand by a jock, followed by a fatphobic remark. Instead, she shares a flirtatious and banterful relationship with the jock character, Nick, who is the Student Body Vice President and her partner on Student Council. They have a relationship, a friendship that transcends typical social boundaries, and Molly even has the upper hand in the power dynamic between the two of them, which makes it all the more interesting. She totally has a crush on him, but she never craves his attention or basks in what little he throws her way. They have an adorable camaraderie that even has him vying for her attention and praise because he acknowledges her worth as a smart, funny and interesting individual.

In the inciting incident, when Molly is in the gender-neutral bathroom (*Yes, Olivia!*) and overhears people speaking about her, she reclaims her power – or tries to – by shrugging off their comments and rubbing it in their faces that she is going to Yale. She refuses to let them make her feel lesser because she is superior to them because of her intellectual status and, in her mind, this trumps their superiority in social status.

When she finds out that one of the mockers, a thin girl who gets called AAA because of her reputation of giving 'roadside assistance' to men in her car, also got into Yale, this throws Molly completely off.

Molly was convinced that she could not be intelligent and accomplished enough to get into a top school while at the same time developing her social relationships and finding her sexual empowerment (outside of masturbation, which she openly talks to Amy about. Again, *YES, Olivia!*). Molly is not shown to be lacking or morally corrupt, she is just shown to be misled. To me, this is a far more nuanced and interesting inciting incident that allows Molly so much more room for development and growth than other films in the same genre, such as *The DUFF*.

Molly and Amy gear up for a wild night, determined to go to a party they don't have the address for, and go to great lengths to find.

After an awkward cab ride with a teacher, a party for no one on a cruise ship, and a murder mystery party that gave them an accidental hallucinogenic trip, Molly and Amy consider giving up and going home. Molly confesses to Amy her crush on Nick, and her wanting to go to the party to see if their flirtatious working relationship could exist and grow outside of the Student Body environment. As soon as Molly acknowledges the crush, she concedes that he probably doesn't fancy her in return.

It's the halfway point of the film, and I hold my breath. So far, I have found this film nothing short of perfect, and I have loved every second of their journey. I wait for Molly to be self-deprecating, and to say out loud that she is not deserving of love because of her looks.

Before she can even get close to this, she is slapped in the face by Amy.

Amy, angrily, pulls up Molly for even daring saying something so negative about herself. She emphatically defends Molly, crushes any hint of self-doubt and proclaims her title of 'best friend' with pride, stating that she will not allow anyone to ever speak that way about someone she loves so much, not even Molly herself.

I gasped.

I was so shocked by the scene that I had to rewind it and watch it again to process what happened. And then came the elation.

What I was expecting to go down was that the Thin Girl Best Friend trope would emerge in Amy. Amy would confirm Molly's acknowledgement of her social standing and her lesser worth as a person because of her size. To see Amy, a Thin Lead stand up so vehemently against this ideology gave me so much joy. It reinforced the power that the wise words of a best friend who loves you can have. It was amazing to see someone use their thin privilege as a way of shielding their plus size best friend from the worst that society has to offer.

I think the reason I was so ready for Molly to continue her train of thought is because I have been Molly many times in my life. I have been confident and capable and assured of my talent and my worth, yet I have still listened to the voices that come to me unbidden and tell me it is not enough. When Amy slapped Molly in the face I felt the sting on my own cheek. I felt the shock of being denied to sink into that place of acceptance. I felt the well of self-pity close over again, and felt my feet on solid ground.

I have known many Amys in my life. Women who love me and see me for everything that I am, fat just being one tiny part of it. Women who stand up for me and to me, who do not let me doubt for a second that I am worthy to be the main character of my story.

In every chapter of this book, I have explored a new way in which society uses the stories we tell and the way we tell them to bring down people who look like me and make us believe that we are not worthy. When you are faced with that ideology daily it's hard to believe with absolute certainty that it's untrue.

When someone, especially a thin person, is willing to stand up for you and remind you to your face that the ideology is wrong; it can help you heal so many old, deep and painful wounds.

So, are you a Molly or are you an Amy? Are you neither? Are you both?

Female friendship is the silver bullet. We live in a patriarchal society, simply being a woman places you in the line of fire of discrimination. How many bad days have been made better by talking to a friend about it?

As women, we are told that our stories are not as worthy or important as stories about men; you just have to look at the list of Best Film winners from the past several decades of the Oscars to see that, but we are the keepers of each other's stories. The things we whisper in the bathroom stalls, our WhatsApp group chats, the secrets we share between our sisters and our friends, our stories that change and save lives. All these stories deserve their space on the big and small screen.

We have a long way to go for women in general, especially for fat women, but can you imagine if for every fat woman wanting to write her story, there was a best friend (of any size) screaming at them that they are worthy? That their story needs to be heard. How many more stories would make it out into the world this way? How many more people would be inspired by seeing these stories? How many more people's lives would be made easier with the ability, confidence and the language to call out bad behaviour and discrimination against plus size bodies in the stories that we see and hear?

This year my best friend and I wrote and performed in a pilot episode for BBC Scotland. The show is about two outrageous friends fast approaching 30 who still act like they are fresh out of university. Although we are a fat and thin duo we are both protagonists, both have our own stakes and wants and needs, both sexually empowered and at absolutely no point is my size, my weight or my body in general used as a tool to inform my character.

I was the one in control, holding the pen, so I got to do things my way. That is the power of writing your own stories.

I never had *Booksmart* when I was a teenager.

I had the *Sisterhood of Travelling Pants*, *Shallow Hal*, *Gilmore Girls* and *Friends* and so many other stories that all had a hand in my development as a human and as someone interested in pursuing a career in film and television as an adult. If I had had *Booksmart* when I was a teenager, I would have understood more the value of who I was as a person and as a friend. I wouldn't have believed that I had to earn my place within my friendship groups by being smart and funny.

I heard somewhere that you should tell the stories that you needed as a child. I needed *Booksmart*. I needed someone fat and beautiful like me to be adventurous, and sexual, and smart, and valued, and the hero of the damn story. I have that now, and I know what my purpose is going forward.

And I am by no means the first person to do this. Award-winning film and television shows featuring fat women have come to light because they have been adapted from the brave autobiographical stories that dared to enter the media space. *My Mad, Fat Diary* is adapted from the diaries of the very real and hilarious Rae Earl, sharing her experiences from when she was a teenager. *Shrill*, the hit American show that was picked up by BBC3, about a plus size woman finding her space is adapted from the book of essays of the same name by Lindy West, sharing her experience as a fat woman and opinion writer for the *New York Times*. I have these real-life role models who have loudly and proudly been themselves and shared their stories unapologetically in the real world. Stories that are so powerful they adapted them for television. Stories that are grounded in reality, in hardship, in experience and in joy.

I hope you have them too, because my story is not your story, and it's not trying to be. But I hope my story and this book holds the door open a little for you to share yours.

There is space for our stories out there.

We deserve to claim our space. We deserve to be seen.

I've had a long time to unpack the damage that was done to me. It's still something I'm working on and it will take a long time, but I will get there. I continue moving towards that place with the help of the women around me; with my friends, my colleagues, and with you.

We'll all keep working on it, getting there and eventually telling stories that we all needed as kids.

If you have ever felt like you are like any of the characters mentioned in this book, and have felt bad about that, you are in no way alone. You are surrounded by people all over the world who have felt it too and you have people who are working to make change.

You have *Booksmart* and films like it. Films out now, films coming out soon, films that haven't been written yet. *Orange is the New Black*. You have Dawn French and the *Vicar of Dibley*.

And you have me.

A babe with a bob-cut and a magnificent bosom.

Working

Speaking

Claiming my Space

Holding the Door Open

A Writer and Filmmaker

An Audience Member

A Friend

• • •

About the Cover Artist

Molly Hankinson is a visual artist from London, currently based in Glasgow. She graduated in Fine Art: Painting and Printmaking from The Glasgow School of Art (2018), and was then awarded the graduate studio residency at SWG3 Studio Warehouse, where she now has her permanent studio. Molly looks at the honest and unapologetic representation of people and communities through an intersectional feminist lens, with an unparalleled and cele-bratory reclamation and ownership of space evident in her work. Incorporating the aesthetics of bright and considered colour placement with use of continuous line, Molly creates 'bold and subtly detailed, inclusive celebrations of feminine vitality'. She works across a broad range of artistic practices, from large-scale mural work, to painting, printmaking, and hand-drawn and digital illustration.

Molly's mural work can be seen across Glasgow and London.

https://www.mollyhankinson.com

About the Cover Artist

FGBF BINGO

Thin Lead (heart)	Physical Ineptitude	Frumpy Costuming	Holding/ Talking Food
Thin Lead Smack Down	*Thin Lead* (heart)	Stating Obvious	Fat Boyfriend
Stating Obvious	Fat Boyfriend	*Thin Lead* (heart)	Physical Ineptitude
Frumpy Costuming	Holding Talking Food	Thin Lead Smack Down	*Thin Lead* (heart)

Just take a photo and play wherever!
Or download from www.tippermuirbooks.co.uk

OTHER TITLES
FROM TIPPERMUIR BOOKS

Spanish Thermopylae (2009)

Battleground Perthshire (2009)

Perth: Street by Street (2012)

Born in Perthshire (2012)

In Spain with Orwell (2013)

Trust (2014)

Perth: As Others Saw Us (2014)

Love All (2015)

A Chocolate Soldier (2016)

The Early Photographers of Perthshire (2016)

Taking Detective Novels Seriously: The Collected Crime
   Reviews of Dorothy L Sayers (2017)

Walking with Ghosts (2017)

No Fair City: Dark Tales from Perth's Past (2017)

The Tale o the Wee Mowdie that wantit tae ken wha keeched
   on his heid (2017)

Hunters: Wee Stories from the Crescent: A Reminiscence of
   Perth's Hunter Crescent (2017)

A Little Book of Carol's (2018)

Flipstones (2018)

Perth: Scott's Fair City: The Fair Maid of Perth &
   Sir Walter Scott – A Celebration & Guided Tour (2018)

God, Hitler, and Lord Peter Wimsey: Selected Essays,
   Speeches and Articles by Dorothy L Sayers (2019)

Perth & Kinross: A Pocket Miscellany: A Companion for
   Visitors and Residents (2019)

The Piper of Tobruk: Pipe Major Robert Roy, MBE, DCM (2019)

The 'Gig Docter o Atholl': Dr William Irvine & The Irvine
   Memorial Hospital (2019)

Afore the Highlands: The Jacobites in Perth, 1715–16 (2019)

'Where Sky and Summit Meet': Flight Over Perthshire –
A History: Tales of Pilots, Airfields, Aeronautical Feats,
& War (2019)

Diverted Traffic (2020)

Authentic Democracy: An Ethical Justification of Anarchism
(2020)

'If Rivers Could Sing': A Scottish River Wildlife Journey.
A Year in the Life of the River Devon as it flows through the
Counties of Perthshire, Kinross-shire & Clackmannanshire
(2020)

A Squatter o Bairnrhymes (2020)

In a Sma Room Songbook: From the Poems by William Soutar
(2020)

The Nicht Afore Christmas: the much-loved yuletide tale in
Scots (2020)

Ice Cold Blood (2021)

The Perth Riverside Nursery & Beyond:
A Spirit of Enterprise and Improvement (2021)

Fatal Duty: The Scottish Police Force to 1952:
Cop Killers, Killer Cops & More (2021)

The Shanter Legacy: The Search for the Grey Mare's Tail (2021)

'Dying to Live': The Story of Grant McIntyre, Covid's Sickest
Patient (2021)

The Black Watch and the Great War (2021)

Beyond the Swelkie: A Collection of Poems & Writings to
Mark the Centenary of George Mackay Brown (2021)

Sweet F.A. (2022)

A War of Two Halves (2022)

A Scottish Wildlife Odyssey (2022)

In the Shadow of Piper Alpha (2022)

Mind the Links: Golf Memories (2022)

Perthshire 101: A Poetic Gazetteer of the Big County (2022)

The Banes o the Turas: An Owersettin in Scots o the Poems bi Pino Mereu scrievit in Tribute tae Hamish Henderson (2022)

FORTHCOMING

William Soutar: Collected Poetry, Volume I (Published Work) (Paul S Philippou (Editor-in-Chief) & Kirsteen McCue and Philippa Osmond-Williams (editors), 2023

William Soutar: Collected Poetry, Volume II (Published Work) (Paul S Philippou (Editor-in-Chief) & Kirsteen McCue and Philippa Osmond-Williams (editors), 2023

Wild Quest Britain: A Nature Journey of Discovery through England, Scotland & Wales – from Lizard Point to Dunnet Head (Keith Broomfield, 2023)

Guid Morning (Lawrence Schimel and Elīna Braslina, Scots translation by Matthew Mackie, 2023)

Madainn Mhath! (Lawrence Schimel and Elīna Braslina, Scottish Gaelic translation by Marcas mac Tuairneir, 2023)

Guid Nicht (Lawrence Schimel and Elīna Braslina, Scots translation by Matthew Mackie, 2023)

Oidhche Mhath! (Lawrence Schimel and Elīna Braslina, Scottish Gaelic translation by Marcas mac Tuairneir, 2023)

The Stone of Destiny and its Historical Journey to Perth Museum (John Hulbert, 2024)

The Mysterious Case of the Stone of Destiny: A Scottish Historical Detective Whodunnit! (David Maule, 2024)

A History of Irish Nationalism and Republicanism in Dundee (c1840 to the Early 1980s) (Ruth Nic Foirbeis, 2023)

The Black Watch from the Crimean War to the Second Boer War (Derek Patrick and Fraser Brown, 2024)

William Soutar: Complete Poetry, Volume III (Unpublished Work) (Paul S Philippou (Editor-in-Chief) & Kirsteen McCue and Philippa Osmond-Williams (editors), 2024)

The Whole Damn Town (Hannah Ballantyne, 2024)

Balkan Rhapsody (Maria Kassimova-Moisset, translated by Iliyana Nedkova Byrne, 2024)

TIPPERMUIR
· BOOKS LIMITED ·

All Tippermuir Books titles are available from bookshops
and online booksellers. They can also be purchased directly
(with free postage & packing (UK only) – minimum charges
for overseas delivery) from **www.tippermuirbooks.co.uk**

Tippermuir Books Ltd can be contacted at
mail@tippermuirbooks.co.uk